# POLYMER CLAY JEWELRY: A BEGINNER'S GUIDE TO CRAFTING STUNNING HANDMADE ACCESSORIES

## STEP-BY-STEP TECHNIQUES, ESSENTIAL TOOLS, AND CREATIVE PROJECTS TO ELEVATE YOUR JEWELRY-MAKING SKILLS

Alinna Brixton

# TABLE OF CONTENT

# CHAPTER 1. INTRODUCTION TO POLYMER CLAY JEWELRY

## UNDERSTANDING POLYMER CLAY: COMPOSITION AND CHARACTERISTICS

Polymer clay is a highly versatile and synthetic modeling material used for crafting jewelry, figurines, home décor, and various art projects. Unlike natural clay, it does not air dry but requires baking at a controlled temperature to harden permanently. This property makes it an excellent medium for jewelry-making, allowing for intricate details, vibrant colors, and durable finished pieces.

**Composition of Polymer Clay**

Polymer clay is made from polyvinyl chloride

(PVC) particles suspended in a plasticizer, which gives it a pliable texture before curing. Additional components such as stabilizers, fillers, and color pigments enhance its performance and aesthetic appeal.

- **Polyvinyl Chloride (PVC):** The primary base material that provides flexibility and durability.
- **Plasticizers:** These ensure the clay remains soft and workable until cured.
- **Stabilizers:** Help maintain the clay's chemical integrity, preventing degradation over time.
- **Fillers:** Used to modify texture and density, affecting how the clay feels and behaves.
- **Pigments and Colorants:** Provide a wide range of vibrant colors, including metallic, translucent, and glow-in-the-dark options.

**Characteristics of Polymer Clay**

Polymer clay possesses several unique properties that make it an ideal choice for jewelry-making and other creative projects.

- **Soft and Workable:** It remains pliable until baked, allowing unlimited working time.
- **Lightweight:** Unlike natural clay or metal, polymer clay jewelry is comfortable to wear.
- **Wide Color Range:** Available in solid, translucent, metallic, and even glow-in-the-dark varieties.
- **Strong and Durable:** When baked correctly, it resists breaking, chipping, or crumbling.
- **Waterproof and Non-Toxic:** Once cured, polymer clay is waterproof and safe for everyday use.
- **Versatile:** Can be blended with other materials such as resin, mica powders, and metal leaf.

**Types of Polymer Clay**

Different brands and formulations of polymer clay offer varying properties suitable for specific projects.

- **Soft Clay:** Easier to manipulate and blend, ideal for beginners.

- **Firm Clay:** Holds fine details better, making it perfect for intricate jewelry and sculpting.
- **Translucent Clay:** Mimics materials like jade, marble, and glass when cured.
- **Glitter and Metallic Clay:** Infused with shimmer particles for an eye-catching effect.
- **Glow-in-the-Dark Clay:** Absorbs light and glows in dark environments, perfect for unique jewelry designs.

## WHY CHOOSE POLYMER CLAY FOR JEWELRY?

Polymer clay has become a popular material for handmade jewelry due to its versatility, ease of use, and affordability. Whether you are a beginner exploring jewelry-making for the first time or a professional artisan looking for a flexible medium, polymer clay offers endless creative possibilities.

### 1. Easy to Work With

Polymer clay is beginner-friendly and requires no specialized equipment to start. Unlike traditional ceramics or metalworking, which demand kilns, torches, or heavy-duty tools, polymer clay can be shaped by hand and cured in a home oven. This accessibility makes it an excellent choice for hobbyists and professional jewelry makers alike.

## 2. Lightweight and Comfortable

One of the most significant advantages of polymer clay is its lightweight nature. Even large statement earrings, chunky necklaces, or bold cuff bracelets made from polymer clay are comfortable to wear for extended periods. This makes it a preferred material for trendy and oversized jewelry designs that wouldn't be practical with metal or stone.

## 3. Wide Range of Colors and Effects

Polymer clay comes in an extensive variety of colors, including solid, translucent, metallic, and pearlized shades. Additionally, colors can be blended to create custom hues and intricate patterns. Techniques like marbling, color gradients, and millefiori can be used to achieve striking visual effects without the need for additional painting.

## 4. Durable and Long-Lasting

Once properly cured, polymer clay is highly durable and resistant to breakage under normal use. Unlike natural clay, which can become brittle if not glazed or fired correctly, polymer clay retains slight flexibility, reducing the risk of cracking. This makes it a reliable material for jewelry that can withstand everyday wear.

## 5. Cost-Effective for All Skill Levels

Compared to metals and gemstones, polymer clay is an inexpensive alternative for jewelry-making. Beginners can start with a small investment, as polymer clay requires minimal tools to create stunning pieces. Professionals can produce high-end, custom jewelry without the high cost of traditional materials.

## 6. Compatible with Mixed Media and Embellishments

Polymer clay works well with a variety of other materials, allowing for endless creativity. You can incorporate:

- Metal components like wire, chains, and bezels
- Resin overlays for a glossy, glass-like finish
- Acrylic paints and mica powders for added color effects
- Gold or silver leaf for a luxurious metallic shine
- Pressed flowers, beads, or fabric textures for unique designs

This adaptability makes polymer clay ideal for experimenting with different styles, from minimalist to bohemian, vintage, or contemporary.

## 7. Simple and Safe Baking Process

Unlike metal clay or ceramics that require specialized kilns, polymer clay hardens at 230°F to 275°F (110°C to 135°C) in a standard home oven. This low-temperature curing process makes it safe for home-based jewelry-making, with no need for industrial equipment.

## 8. Environmentally Conscious and Non-Toxic Options

Many polymer clay brands are non-toxic and safe for use, even by children under supervision.

Additionally, because polymer clay is long-lasting and does not degrade easily, it reduces waste compared to fast-fashion accessories that wear out quickly. Some artisans also use polymer clay as an alternative to more environmentally damaging jewelry materials.

## 9. Endless Design Possibilities

With polymer clay, the creative potential is limitless. Artists can sculpt, carve, mold, and texture the clay to create:

- Delicate floral earrings
- Geometric statement pieces
- Intricate millefiori patterns
- Faux gemstones and mineral effects
- Bohemian and nature-inspired pendants

No other jewelry material offers such a combination of sculpting freedom, vibrant color possibilities, and ease of handling.

## 10. Market Demand and Handmade Appeal

Handmade polymer clay jewelry has surged in popularity due to its customizable nature. Buyers appreciate one-of-a-kind, handcrafted pieces, and many artisans successfully sell polymer clay jewelry through online platforms like Etsy, craft fairs, and boutique stores. With the right branding and craftsmanship, polymer clay jewelry can become a profitable business.

## EXPLORING STYLES: FROM MINIMALIST TO STATEMENT PIECES

Polymer clay jewelry offers a vast range of design possibilities, from sleek, understated pieces to bold, eye-catching accessories. Whether you prefer delicate everyday wear or dramatic statement pieces, polymer clay provides the flexibility to bring any style to life. Understanding different jewelry styles will help you determine your creative direction and cater to various fashion preferences.

### 1. Minimalist Jewelry: Subtle and Elegant

Minimalist jewelry is characterized by clean lines, simple shapes, and a refined aesthetic. This style appeals to those who appreciate understated elegance and versatile accessories that complement any outfit.

**Common Features of Minimalist Polymer Clay Jewelry:**

- Geometric shapes like circles, squares, and ovals
- Neutral and monochromatic color palettes
- Smooth, matte, or lightly textured surfaces
- Small, lightweight pieces such as stud earrings, dainty pendants, and thin bangles
- Minimal embellishments for a sleek, modern look

Minimalist polymer clay jewelry is ideal for everyday wear and pairs well with casual, professional, and formal attire.

**2. Bohemian (Boho) Jewelry: Free-Spirited and Artistic**

Bohemian jewelry is inspired by nature, culture, and artistic expression. This style embraces earthy tones, organic shapes, and intricate details to create a relaxed, free-spirited look.

**Common Features of Boho Polymer Clay Jewelry:**

- Natural textures such as faux wood, stone, or leather finishes
- Hand-sculpted floral or nature-inspired motifs
- Earthy and warm color tones, often blended in marbled or ombre effects
- Tassels, feathers, and mixed media elements like beads and metal charms
- Asymmetrical or layered designs for a dynamic look

Boho polymer clay jewelry is perfect for festival wear, casual outfits, and artistic fashion statements.

### 3. Statement Jewelry: Bold and Dramatic

Statement jewelry is designed to be the focal point of an outfit, featuring large-scale designs, vibrant colors, and unique textures. This style is ideal for those who want their accessories to stand out.

**Common Features of Statement Polymer Clay Jewelry:**

- Oversized earrings, chunky necklaces, and bold rings
- Bright, saturated colors and striking patterns
- Textured surfaces, embossed designs, or sculpted details
- Contrasting elements such as metallic foils, resin overlays, or abstract shapes
- Layered or three-dimensional designs for added depth

Statement polymer clay jewelry is often worn for special occasions, fashion-forward outfits, and artistic self-expression.

**4. Vintage and Retro Jewelry: Nostalgic and Classic**

Vintage-inspired polymer clay jewelry incorporates design elements from past eras, such as the Art Deco, Victorian, or Mid-Century Modern periods. Retro styles, on the other hand, embrace bold patterns and bright colors reminiscent of the 1960s and 1980s.

**Common Features of Vintage and Retro Polymer Clay Jewelry:**

- Ornate details such as filigree patterns, cameos, or lace textures
- Pastel tones, floral motifs, and antique-inspired embellishments
- Gold or bronze accents for a classic, aged look
- Graphic patterns, polka dots, and bold color blocking for retro appeal
- Glossy finishes or resin coatings to mimic enamel jewelry

Vintage and retro polymer clay jewelry appeals to those who love timeless elegance or playful, nostalgic designs.

**5. Modern and Abstract Jewelry: Innovative and Unique**

Modern polymer clay jewelry often features experimental shapes, unconventional color combinations, and cutting-edge techniques.

Abstract designs push the boundaries of traditional jewelry, making them perfect for artistic expression.

**Common Features of Modern and Abstract Polymer Clay Jewelry:**

- Unusual, asymmetric forms that defy conventional design rules
- Experimental textures, such as crumpled, folded, or sculpted surfaces
- High-contrast color palettes, including black-and-white or neon combinations
- Layered, mixed-media elements for a futuristic aesthetic
- Bold architectural shapes that resemble sculpture or contemporary art

This style is ideal for those who enjoy innovative, high-fashion accessories that make a creative statement.

**Choosing the Right Style for You**

When designing polymer clay jewelry, consider your personal preferences, target audience, and intended use. Some creators specialize in a single style, while others blend multiple elements to develop a signature look. Whether you prefer sleek minimalism or daring statement pieces, polymer clay provides the freedom to experiment and craft jewelry that reflects your artistic vision.

## ESSENTIAL TOOLS AND MATERIALS FOR BEGINNERS

Getting started with polymer clay jewelry requires a few basic tools and materials. While advanced techniques may involve specialized equipment, beginners can create high-quality pieces with simple and affordable supplies. Understanding the essential tools will help you work efficiently and achieve professional-looking results.

**1. Polymer Clay: Choosing the Right Type**

Polymer clay comes in different brands and formulations, each with unique properties. Some clays are softer and easier to shape, while others are firmer and better suited for intricate designs.

**Popular Polymer Clay Brands:**

- **Sculpey Premo** – Durable, flexible, and great for detailed work

- **FIMO Professional** – Firm texture, ideal for precise sculpting

- **Cernit** – Translucent and excellent for faux gemstone effects

- **Kato Polyclay** – Strong, resistant to breakage, and preferred by professionals

- **Sculpey Soufflé** – Soft, lightweight, and slightly suede-like in texture

Beginners should start with a brand that is easy to condition and holds its shape well after baking.

## 2. Basic Tools for Shaping and Cutting

To create well-defined polymer clay jewelry, you need tools that help you cut, shape, and refine your designs.

- **Acrylic Rolling Pin or Pasta Machine** – For flattening and conditioning clay

- **Clay Blades** – Flexible and rigid blades for clean, precise cuts
- **Needle Tool or Pin** – For making small holes and adding fine details
- **Cookie Cutters or Shape Templates** – For consistent shapes and symmetrical designs
- **Dotting Tools or Ball Styluses** – For texturing and smoothing surfaces
- **X-Acto Knife or Precision Blade** – For intricate cuts and sharp edges

## 3. Work Surface and Handling Tools

A smooth, non-stick surface is essential to prevent clay from sticking or picking up dust.

- **Glass, Ceramic Tile, or Acrylic Sheet** – Provides a clean and sturdy workspace
- **Baking Paper or Wax Paper** – Protects surfaces from clay residue
- **Cornstarch or Baby Powder** – Prevents clay from sticking to molds and tools
- **Latex or Nitrile Gloves** – Helps avoid fingerprints and keeps the clay clean

## 4. Texturing and Finishing Tools

Adding texture and patterns can enhance the look of polymer clay jewelry.

- **Rubber Stamps and Texture Sheets** – Imprint decorative patterns onto clay
- **Sandpaper (400-1000 Grit)** – Smooths out rough edges after baking
- **Buffing Cloth or Dremel Tool** – Polishes surfaces for a professional finish
- **Gloss or Matte Varnish** – Seals and protects finished jewelry

## 5. Baking and Curing Essentials

Polymer clay needs to be baked at specific temperatures to harden properly. Using the right baking setup ensures durability and prevents burning.

- **Home Oven or Toaster Oven** – Must maintain a stable temperature between 230°F - 275°F (110°C - 135°C)
- **Oven Thermometer** – Prevents overheating and ensures accurate baking temperatures

- **Ceramic Tile or Glass Baking Surface** – Provides even heat distribution
- **Aluminum Foil Tent or Cardstock** – Protects clay from direct heat to prevent darkening

## 6. Jewelry Findings and Assembly Tools

To turn polymer clay pieces into wearable jewelry, you need metal components and assembly tools.

- **Jump Rings, Earring Hooks, and Clasps** – Essential for connecting jewelry pieces
- **Eye Pins and Head Pins** – For securing beads and dangles
- **Jewelry Pliers (Round Nose and Flat Nose)** – For bending and assembling metal findings
- **Strong Adhesive (E6000 or Super Glue)** – For attaching metal parts to clay

## 7. Optional Additives and Decorative Elements

Enhance your jewelry designs with additional materials and embellishments.

- **Mica Powder or Metallic Foil** – Adds shimmer and depth

- **Acrylic or Alcohol Inks** – For painting and unique surface effects
- **Resin or UV Resin** – Creates a glossy, glass-like finish
- **Glitter, Dried Flowers, or Beads** – Adds texture and visual interest

# CHAPTER 2. MASTERING POLYMER CLAY TECHNIQUES

## CONDITIONING AND SOFTENING CLAY PROPERLY

Conditioning polymer clay is an essential step before using with it. A properly conditioned clay is easier to shape, blend, and manipulate, and it ensures that your jewelry pieces are durable and smooth after baking. If the clay is not properly conditioned, it can be brittle, difficult to work with, or may not bake evenly. Here's how to condition and soften polymer clay for optimal results.

**1. Why Conditioning is Important**

Conditioning polymer clay serves several purposes:

- **Softens the Clay:** Polymer clay can be firm when first removed from the package, especially if it's been sitting for a while. Softening it makes it more pliable and easier to work with.

- **Ensures Even Consistency:** Conditioning helps evenly distribute the plasticizers throughout the clay, reducing air bubbles and creating a consistent texture.
- **Improves Workability:** Well-conditioned clay is smoother and easier to mold, sculpt, and blend, ensuring your designs hold their shape.

## 2. Methods for Conditioning Polymer Clay

There are different techniques for conditioning clay, each suited to the tools and time available.

### Manual Conditioning

This is the simplest method and requires no additional tools other than your hands. It's ideal for small batches of clay.

### Kneading by Hand:

- Start by breaking the clay into smaller pieces if you are working with a large block.
- Begin kneading the clay in your hands, rolling and pressing it between your palms, much like dough.

- As you knead, you'll feel the clay become softer and more pliable. If it sticks to your hands, lightly dust your hands with cornstarch or baby powder to prevent it from getting too sticky.
- Continue kneading for around 5-10 minutes, or until the clay is smooth and flexible.

**Pasta Machine Conditioning**

A pasta machine is an excellent tool for conditioning large amounts of clay quickly and evenly. This method is especially useful for getting a consistent texture.

**Set the Pasta Machine to a Thick Setting:**

- Begin by rolling the polymer clay into a small log or ball.
- Feed the clay through the pasta machine, using the thickest setting.
- Fold the clay in half and pass it through again. Repeat this process until the clay becomes smooth, soft, and pliable.

- Gradually reduce the thickness setting as the clay softens. This helps ensure that the clay is thoroughly conditioned and free of air bubbles.

**Using a Roller or Acrylic Pin**

A roller or acrylic pin can also help soften polymer clay, especially if you're conditioning smaller amounts or preparing sheets of clay for larger projects.

**Roll Out the Clay:**

- Flatten the clay with a rolling pin, pressing evenly as you go.
- Fold and roll the clay multiple times to work the plasticizers into the material.
- This method works similarly to the pasta machine, although it may require more effort for even conditioning.

**3. Dealing with Hard Clay**

If the polymer clay is too hard or crumbly, it may need extra effort to soften.

**Use Softening Agents:**

- For very hard clay, you can mix in a small amount of clay softener (available at craft stores). This is a liquid designed to soften the clay and improve its flexibility.
- You can also use liquid polymer clay, which helps in softening and adding moisture back into the clay without affecting its integrity.
- If using softeners or liquid clay, only add a few drops at a time, as too much will make the clay too sticky.

**Warm Up the Clay:**

- If your clay is too firm because of cold temperatures, warm it up slightly by placing it in a warm, but not hot, area or using a hairdryer on a low setting. Be cautious not to melt or overheat the clay.

**4. Signs of Properly Conditioned Clay**

Properly conditioned polymer clay should have the following qualities:

- **Smooth Texture:** There should be no lumps, cracks, or visible streaks in the clay.
- **Softness:** The clay should be flexible and easy to shape without cracking or breaking.
- **Even Consistency:** It should feel like a soft, pliable dough, with no dry spots or air pockets.
- **No Stickiness:** When you handle the clay, it should not stick excessively to your fingers or tools (light dusting with cornstarch can prevent this if needed).

## 5. What to Do if Clay Becomes Too Soft or Sticky

If your polymer clay becomes too soft or sticky after conditioning, it can be challenging to work with. To solve this, follow these steps:

- **Use Cornstarch or Baby Powder:** Lightly dust the clay with cornstarch or baby powder to absorb excess moisture.
- **Chill the Clay:** Wrap the clay in plastic wrap and place it in the refrigerator for 15-30 minutes to firm it up.

- **Condition Again:** If necessary, recondition the clay by kneading or passing it through the pasta machine again to bring it back to the right consistency.

## 6. Storage Tips for Polymer Clay

Once conditioned, store your polymer clay in airtight containers or plastic wrap to prevent it from drying out. You can refrigerate the clay to keep it at an ideal consistency for longer, but be sure to bring it to room temperature before using it again.

## Conclusion

Proper conditioning is the foundation of successful polymer clay jewelry making. Whether you're working by hand, with a pasta machine, or using softening agents, ensuring your clay is smooth, pliable, and evenly conditioned will make your projects easier and your results more professional. Experiment with different conditioning methods and find the one that works best for your creative process.

# SHAPING AND SCULPTING: BASIC FORMS AND FREEHAND DESIGNS

Shaping and sculpting are vital techniques in polymer clay jewelry making. Mastering these skills allows you to create both structured forms and freehand, organic designs. Whether you're making simple shapes like beads or intricate freeform pieces, understanding how to manipulate polymer clay will help you produce high-quality, creative jewelry.

## 1. Understanding Basic Forms

The foundation of many polymer clay designs lies in the ability to shape basic forms. These simple structures can be modified and combined in countless ways to create complex jewelry pieces.

**Common Basic Forms:**

- **Balls:** The simplest form, great for creating beads, charms, or cabochons.
- **Cylinders:** Can be used for beads, pendants, or any elongated designs.

- **Cubes and Rectangles:** Useful for creating geometric shapes, pendants, or earrings.
- **Flattened Shapes:** Pressing the clay into discs, ovals, or rectangles is a good starting point for earrings, brooches, or layered designs.
- **Teardrops:** Excellent for creating dangling earrings or pendants with an elegant, curved look.
- **Spheres and Cones:** Often used for beads or 3D sculptural designs.

**Techniques for Shaping Basic Forms:**

- **Rolling by Hand:** Roll the clay between your palms or fingers to form smooth balls or cylinders. Use gentle pressure to ensure the clay is evenly shaped.
- **Using Molds:** For consistent shapes, you can use silicone molds or cookie cutters to press out basic shapes. This is especially useful for making multiple pieces at once, such as uniform beads.

- **Slicing and Cutting:** If you need uniform discs or flat shapes, use a blade or an acrylic rolling pin to flatten the clay, then slice it into the desired size.
- **Pushing and Pinching:** Gently pinch, push, or roll the clay to transform its shape into something more complex, like cones, pointed tips, or custom designs.

## 2. Freehand Sculpting: Embracing Organic Shapes

While basic forms are great building blocks, freehand sculpting gives you the flexibility to create more intricate and unique jewelry designs. Freehand designs allow you to experiment with texture, shapes, and movement, producing truly one-of-a-kind pieces.

### Techniques for Freehand Sculpting:

- **Pinching and Pulling:** For freeform shapes, use your fingers to pinch, pull, and stretch the clay. Pinching is useful for creating points, curls, or petal-like structures. This technique works well for making flowers, leaves, and abstract designs.

- **Sculpting with Tools:** Use sculpting tools such as needles, dotting tools, or even knitting needles to add texture and refine the shape. These tools can help you create delicate details like veins in leaves, hairlines in faces, or patterns in flowers.

- **Slicing and Layering:** To add dimension, slice thin sheets of clay and stack them to build up layers. You can also use this method to make marbled effects or to create layered patterns like flowers or mandalas.

- **Rolling Thin Sheets:** Roll out clay into very thin sheets, then use them to add elements like tiny petals, leaves, or other organic designs. Thin sheets can also be used to make intricate canes or geometric patterns.

- **Twisting and Coiling:** Twist and coil thin ropes of clay to create spirals, swirls, and other flowing designs. This technique works particularly well for adding accents to earrings, necklaces, or rings.

- **Using a Dremel or Clay Extruder:** If you want to create long, thin shapes like wires or rods, a clay extruder can help you achieve uniform strands, which can be twisted or braided into intricate designs. A Dremel tool is excellent for smoothing and refining shapes or adding surface texture.

### 3. Adding Texture to Freehand Designs

Texture can transform a simple piece into something striking and unique. There are several methods for adding texture to your freehand designs.

### Texturing Methods:

- **Using Household Items:** Simple objects like fabric, lace, leaves, or even kitchen utensils can add interesting textures to your clay. Press these items gently into the surface of the clay to create unique patterns.

- **Rubber Stamps and Texture Sheets:** For more detailed patterns, use rubber stamps or textured sheets designed for polymer clay. Pressing these into the clay creates consistent textures that can be used for anything from elegant designs to more abstract, organic looks.

- **Needle Tool or Forks:** Using a fine needle or a fork to add lines, dots, and impressions is an easy way to add texture to freeform sculptures. These tools are great for creating patterns like wood grain or subtle detailing on flower petals.

## 4. Combining Basic Forms and Freehand Designs

One of the most effective ways to create unique polymer clay jewelry is to combine basic shapes with freehand sculpting. For instance, start with a simple cylindrical bead and then add sculpted, freeform leaves around it. This approach allows you to blend the structural simplicity of basic forms with the artistic freedom of freehand design.

**Examples of Combining Techniques:**

- **Beads with Sculpted Accents:** Begin with a smooth ball or cylinder and then add sculpted flowers, leaves, or other elements.

- **Pendants with Intricate Sculpting:** A simple oval or square base can be sculpted into a flower, face, or nature-inspired design, creating a unique pendant.

- **Layered Freehand Designs:** Combine thin layers of freehand-cut clay, texture, and basic shapes to create 3D designs.

- **Geometric and Organic Fusion:** Incorporate geometric elements like squares, triangles, and circles into a freeform piece, creating a balanced and artistic contrast.

## 5. Tips for Perfecting Your Shaping and Sculpting Skills

- **Work with Small Pieces:** Start by shaping small portions of clay so you can focus on details and practice specific techniques.

- **Practice Symmetry:** If your designs need to be symmetrical (e.g., earrings), use a ruler or template to help guide you in creating uniform pieces.

- **Keep Your Tools Clean:** Clean your sculpting tools frequently to avoid transferring unwanted clay colors or textures onto your designs.

- **Take Your Time:** Freehand sculpting can be a delicate process, so allow yourself the time to experiment and refine your designs.

### 6. 5 Simple Beginner Projects

1. **Basic Bead Necklace:**

   Create smooth, round beads in your choice of colors. String them together for a simple yet elegant necklace. Add small sculpted details like leaves or flowers for added flair.

2. **Flower Earrings:**

   Shape small discs of polymer clay into petal shapes, and layer them to form flowers. Attach an earring hook or stud to complete the pair.

3. **Textured Pendant:**

   Use a simple oval base and add texture by pressing fabric or a textured sheet into the surface. After baking, add a jump ring to turn it into a pendant.

4. **Twisted Ring:**

   Roll thin strands of clay and twist them together to create a simple but stylish ring. Bake the ring and add a glossy finish for a polished look.

5. **Abstract Brooch:**

   Start with a flat, circular base and freehand sculpt shapes like spirals, dots, or small flowers. Attach a brooch pin to the back for a creative and wearable accessory.

**Conclusion**

Shaping and sculpting are at the heart of polymer clay jewelry making. Whether you are working with basic forms or creating freehand, organic designs, these techniques allow for endless creative possibilities. Start with simple shapes, practice freehand sculpting, and gradually build your skills to create intricate and beautiful jewelry pieces. With time and patience, you'll be able to bring your ideas to life and create unique, one-of-a-kind designs.

## BLENDING COLORS AND CREATING CUSTOM SHADES

Color is one of the most exciting aspects of polymer clay jewelry making. The ability to blend different hues and create custom shades allows for endless creative possibilities. Whether you're making subtle, harmonious designs or bold, vibrant pieces, understanding how to mix and blend colors will elevate your work to the next level. This section will explore the basics of color blending, tips for creating custom shades, and techniques for achieving unique color effects.

### 1. Understanding Polymer Clay Colors

Polymer clay comes in a wide range of pre-made colors, including vibrant hues, metallics, pastels, and more. However, the beauty of polymer clay lies in its versatility — you can combine different colors to create your own custom palette. To get started, it's important to understand the properties of the clay and how colors interact with each other.

**Types of Polymer Clay Colors:**

- **Solid Colors:** Most polymer clays come in solid, uniform colors. These are often used as the base for mixing and creating custom shades.

- **Translucent Clay:** This type of clay is semi-transparent and can be mixed with opaque colors to create lighter, more delicate tones or to add a glossy finish to designs.

- **Metallic and Pearlized Colors:** These clays contain mica powders or metallic elements that give them a shiny, reflective quality. These are often used for accents and creating eye-catching details.

- **Neon and Fluorescent Colors:** Bright and bold, these colors can be mixed with others to create striking, vibrant combinations.

Understanding these options allows you to determine which colors will suit your design style and vision.

## 2. The Basics of Color Blending

Blending polymer clay colors involves mixing two or more colors to create a new, custom shade. It's a simple process that can produce stunning effects in your jewelry pieces.

**Basic Color Mixing Techniques:**

- **Kneading:** To blend colors effectively, knead the clay thoroughly until the colors are completely integrated. You can either blend by hand or use a pasta machine for a more consistent result.

- **Roll and Fold Method:** Roll each color into a snake or log shape, then fold them together. Repeat the process of rolling and folding until the colors blend seamlessly.

- **Swirling:** For a marbled effect, mix two or more colors together by twisting and swirling them. This creates beautiful, unpredictable patterns in your clay.

- **Layering:** Lay down a thin sheet of one color and then place another color on top. Use a rolling pin or pasta machine to gently flatten and blend the colors.

**Achieving the Desired Effect:**

- **Gradients:** Create a smooth gradient by blending one color into another. Start with two different colors and gradually mix them to create a smooth transition between them. This works well for creating ombre effects or color transitions in your jewelry.

- **Marmalade/Swirl Effect:** To create a marmalade or swirling effect, blend two or more colors but do not overwork them. This keeps the color separation intact, giving you a swirl pattern that looks natural and flowing.

- **Speckled or Dappled Effect:** Use a small amount of contrasting color, knead it lightly into the base color, and then roll it out. The color will appear in small, random specks throughout the design.

## 3. Creating Custom Shades

Creating custom shades of polymer clay allows you to craft unique colors that aren't available in pre-made options. Here are some ways to make your own shades and modify existing ones to match your vision.

**Mixing Basic Colors:**

- **Primary Colors:** Mixing primary colors (red, yellow, and blue) in different proportions allows you to create any color you want. For example, mixing red and yellow creates orange, while mixing yellow and blue creates green.

- **Adding White or Black:** To adjust the intensity of your color, you can add white to lighten it or black to darken it. Just a small amount can drastically change the shade.

- **Complementary Colors:** Mixing complementary colors — those that are opposite on the color wheel — will neutralize the color and create muted or earthy tones. For example, mixing green with red will result in a brownish shade.

**Creating Custom Metallics or Pearls:**

- **Metallics:** Combine metallic polymer clay with regular clays to create unique shimmering effects. Experiment with gold, silver, copper, and other metallic clays to create custom accents or highlights for your jewelry.

- **Pearl Effects:** Mix pearlized clay with a base color to create an iridescent or lustrous finish. You can also mix pearl clay with translucent clay to give your designs a soft, ethereal glow.

**Experimenting with Color Combinations:**

- **Monochromatic Palette:** Create designs that use various shades of a single color. This allows you to play with different tones and depths of the same hue, such as light pink, dark pink, and coral.

- **Analogous Color Scheme:** Use colors that are next to each other on the color wheel, such as blue, green, and yellow. This creates a harmonious, soothing palette.

- **Triadic Color Scheme:** Choose three colors that are evenly spaced on the color wheel, like red, blue, and yellow. This creates a balanced and vibrant combination.

**4. Creating Special Effects with Colors**

Adding special effects to your polymer clay designs enhances the visual impact of your jewelry. These techniques can be used to create stunning, eye-catching pieces that stand out.

**Incorporating Metallic or Pearl Pigments:**

- **Shiny Accents:** Use metallic clay or powders to add highlights and accents to your pieces. Gold or silver detailing can transform a simple design into something striking and elegant.

- **Layered Textures:** Layer metallic clays with solid clays to create depth and dimension. This can be particularly effective for creating jewelry pieces with multiple layers or textures.

**Creating Faded or Distressed Effects:**

- **Fading or Ombre Effects:** By blending colors smoothly, you can create a gradient effect that fades from dark to light. This is perfect for creating necklaces, bracelets, or earrings with a dynamic look.

- **Distressed or Aged Look:** To achieve a vintage, worn look, mix clay with chalks or pastels. Rub them into the surface of your piece after baking to add an aged, rustic appearance.

**Creating Faux Stone Effects:**

- **Marble or Agate:** Mixing two colors and rolling them together can create a marble effect. You can also swirl two colors to replicate agate or stone patterns.

- **Wood Grain:** Mix a translucent base color with tiny strands of another color to simulate wood grain, which can be used for earthy, nature-inspired designs.

## 5. Troubleshooting Common Color Blending Issues

While color blending is fun and rewarding, there are a few challenges that beginners may encounter. Here are some common issues and tips for resolving them.

- **Overmixing:** If you mix your colors too much, you may lose the integrity of the design. Be mindful of the amount of kneading or twisting you do, especially when creating marbled or swirled effects.

- **Colors Becoming Muddy:** Some color combinations can result in muddy, unappealing shades. To avoid this, test your color blends on a small piece of clay before committing to a larger project.

- **Clay Becoming Too Soft:** When mixing colors, the clay may soften and become too sticky, making it harder to work with. If this happens, try chilling your clay in the refrigerator for a few minutes or adding a bit of cornstarch to help firm it up.

## 6. Five Simple Beginner Projects to Explore Color Blending

1. **Color Gradient Earrings:** Create a pair of earrings that transition from light to dark shades of the same color. Use a rolling pin to blend the colors smoothly for a beautiful ombre effect.

2. **Marbled Pendant Necklace:** Mix two or more colors to create a marble effect, then use a cookie cutter to shape the pendant. Finish with a jump ring and chain.

3. **Metallic Accented Bracelet:** Use a base color like black or white and add metallic accents for a chic, modern look. Use a rolling pin to flatten the clay and then cut out geometric shapes for a statement bracelet.

4. **Two-Tone Beads:** Blend two colors together and form smooth beads. Experiment with marbling, swirls, or simple two-tone designs.

5. **Faux Agate Ring:** Create a faux agate design by swirling two colors of clay together. Roll the mixture into a flat, oval shape, then bake and attach a ring base for a beautiful gemstone-inspired ring.

## SURFACE TEXTURING AND PATTERN TECHNIQUES

Surface texture and patterns are essential techniques in polymer clay jewelry making. They allow you to add depth, visual interest, and dimension to your designs, transforming them from simple shapes into stunning, one-of-a-kind pieces. Whether you want to create smooth, polished surfaces or intricate textures that mimic the look of fabric, stone, or metal, mastering surface texturing and pattern techniques is crucial for elevating your work. In this section, we will explore different methods for adding texture and patterns to polymer clay and how to incorporate them into your jewelry designs.

# 1. Understanding the Role of Texture in Jewelry Design

Texture plays a key role in polymer clay jewelry because it adds tactile interest and enhances the visual appeal of a piece. By manipulating the surface of the clay, you can achieve a variety of effects, from subtle patterns to bold, statement-making designs. Texture also helps highlight the colors and materials you've used, drawing attention to the details of your jewelry.

**Why Texture Matters:**

- **Visual Appeal:** Textured surfaces catch the light in different ways, creating shadows and highlights that add dimension to your design.
- **Tactile Sensation:** Texture can make your jewelry feel more engaging when worn, giving it a pleasant tactile quality.
- **Style and Uniqueness:** The type of texture you apply can dramatically affect the style of the piece. Whether it's a smooth, polished finish for a sleek modern look or a rough, organic texture

for a bohemian vibe, texture sets the mood of the jewelry.

## 2. Simple Techniques for Adding Texture to Polymer Clay

There are many ways to create textures on polymer clay, from using everyday items to investing in specialized tools. The following techniques are easy to master and will help you achieve a variety of textured surfaces.

### Using Household Items:

- **Fabric or Lace:** You can press fabric, lace, or textured paper into the surface of the clay to create a delicate pattern. Simply roll out your clay, place the fabric or lace on top, and gently press it down. Peel the fabric away to reveal the texture left behind.

- **Found Objects:** Many common objects can be used to create textures on polymer clay. Examples include a fork, a toothbrush, a rubber stamp, or even a piece of wire mesh. Experiment with different objects to create interesting patterns, from fine lines to geometric shapes.

- **Textured Rolling Pins:** Rolling pins with engraved patterns can be rolled over your polymer clay to impress texture onto the surface. These are especially useful for creating repetitive patterns such as floral designs, brick textures, or wood grain.

## Using Stamps and Molds:

- **Rubber Stamps:** Rubber stamps can be used to create intricate patterns and designs on polymer clay. Simply press the stamp onto the clay to transfer the design. This technique works especially well for creating detailed, repeating patterns.
- **Molds:** Silicone molds allow you to create 3D textures and patterns. Simply press a piece of clay into the mold, and once it's removed, you'll have an embossed design that can be incorporated into your jewelry.

**Impression Tools:**

- **Texturing Tools:** Specialized texturing tools, such as metal scrapers, needle tools, and combs, can be used to carve, scratch, and shape your polymer clay. These tools are perfect for creating more detailed textures like crosshatching, dots, or wavy lines.

- **Brayers and Presses:** A brayer (small rolling pin) or press can be used to gently flatten the surface of the clay, which can reveal an underlying texture or help you create an even finish. You can also use these tools in combination with textures from fabrics, lace, or textured surfaces.

## 3. Creating Patterns Through Stamping and Imprinting

Stamping and imprinting are popular techniques for adding detailed patterns to polymer clay. Both methods are relatively simple to execute and can produce stunning results that bring depth to your jewelry.

**Stamping:** Stamping involves pressing a rubber or acrylic stamp into polymer clay to transfer a pattern or image. The key to successful stamping is to apply even pressure while ensuring that the clay remains firm enough to retain the design.

- **Rubber Stamps:** Using rubber stamps with fine details, such as flowers or geometric shapes, can create an elegant effect. Experiment with different stamp designs to achieve unique results.

- **Custom Stamps:** You can also make your own stamps by carving simple patterns or shapes into rubber, polymer clay, or even wood. This allows you to create completely original designs for your jewelry pieces.

**Imprinting:** Imprinting is a technique in which you press an object, texture, or pattern into the surface of the clay, leaving an impression. Objects like coins, shells, and other textured surfaces work well for creating distinctive patterns.

- **Nature Imprints:** Pressing natural items like leaves, flowers, and seashells into clay can create beautiful organic patterns. For a rustic, natural effect, this technique is perfect for jewelry that evokes earthy, bohemian vibes.

- **Geometric Imprints:** Use stencils or geometric objects like rulers, string, or wire to create precise, clean lines and shapes that add a contemporary, structured look to your pieces.

## 4. Advanced Surface Techniques

Once you've mastered basic texturing, you can experiment with more advanced techniques to add complex details and visual interest to your designs. These methods may require some practice but will allow you to produce truly unique, professional-looking jewelry.

**Carving and Etching:** Carving and etching allow you to add intricate details to the surface of polymer clay. By using sharp tools such as X-Acto knives, dental tools, or needle tools, you can carve out patterns, symbols, or textures into the clay's surface.

- **Carving Designs:** Draw or sketch a design on your clay using a pencil, and then carefully carve along the lines to create a raised or recessed design.

- **Etching:** For etching, apply a thin layer of liquid clay to your design, and then use a sharp tool to etch into the surface. Etching gives your designs a more textured, dramatic effect.

**Sanding and Polishing:** Once you've created your textured designs, sanding and polishing can refine the surface, creating a smooth, shiny finish that enhances the texture's visual appeal. Sanding helps remove any rough edges, while polishing brings out the vibrancy of the color and texture.

- **Wet Sanding:** After baking, wet sand your clay with fine-grit sandpaper to smooth the surface. Start with a coarse grit and move to a finer grit for a polished finish.

- **Buffing:** Use a soft cloth or a buffing wheel to polish the surface of your clay pieces. This will give your jewelry a professional shine, making the textures pop.

**Foil and Leaf Embellishments:** For a high-end, decorative touch, you can add metallic foil or gold leaf to the textured surface of your polymer clay. Foil can be applied by pressing it into the clay's surface before baking, leaving a shiny, metallic finish that contrasts beautifully with the matte texture.

## 5. 5 Simple Beginner Projects for Surface Texturing and Pattern Techniques

1. **Textured Earrings:** Use a textured rolling pin to create a subtle pattern on flat clay discs. Cut them into earring shapes, add hooks, and bake for simple yet elegant textured earrings.

2. **Stamped Pendant Necklace:** Press a rubber stamp into the surface of polymer clay to create an intricate design. Cut out a pendant shape, bake it, and add a chain for a chic necklace.

3. **Imprinted Cuff Bracelet:** Press a nature-inspired object, such as a leaf, into a flat piece of clay to create an organic texture. Form the clay into a cuff bracelet shape and bake it for a unique, earthy look.

4. **Carved Ring:** Use carving tools to create a detailed, etched design on a polymer clay ring band. Sand the surface and add a coat of glaze for a polished finish.

5. **Geometric Brooch:** Use a geometric object like a stencil or a textured roller to create sharp, clean patterns on polymer clay. Cut out geometric shapes and assemble them into a stylish brooch.

**Conclusion**

Surface texturing and pattern techniques are indispensable tools in the polymer clay jewelry maker's toolkit. They not only enhance the aesthetic appeal of your designs but also allow you to experiment with texture, depth, and complexity. By mastering these techniques, you can create jewelry pieces that are truly one-of-a-kind, whether you're working with simple patterns or more advanced carving and etching. With a bit of practice and creativity, you'll be able to transform your polymer clay into stunning works of art.

# CHAPTER 3. ESSENTIAL BAKING AND CURING METHODS

## CHOOSING THE RIGHT TEMPERATURE AND TIME FOR DIFFERENT CLAY BRANDS

When working with polymer clay, the proper baking process is essential to achieving durable, high-quality pieces. However, each polymer clay brand has its own recommended temperature and baking time, and it's crucial to follow these guidelines for the best results. Understanding the differences in how various clay brands cure will help you prevent common issues such as cracking, burning, or under-curing.

In this section, we will explore the factors that influence baking time and temperature, the recommended baking guidelines for different polymer clay brands, and tips for getting the best results from your clay.

# 1. Understanding the Importance of Temperature and Time

Baking polymer clay at the correct temperature and for the appropriate amount of time ensures that it becomes hard and durable, ready for use in jewelry making. If the temperature is too high, the clay may burn or become discoloured. If the temperature is too low, the clay may remain soft and fragile, which could compromise the structure of your designs.

## Key Considerations:

- **Clay Composition:** Different brands of polymer clay use varying formulations, which affects how they cure. Some clays require lower baking temperatures, while others may need slightly higher temperatures for optimal results.

- **Clay Thickness:** The thickness of your pieces also plays a role in baking time. Thicker pieces need more time to fully cure, while thinner pieces can bake more quickly.

- **Oven Type:** Whether you're using a conventional oven, a toaster oven, or a convection oven, the heat distribution can vary. It's important to monitor your oven's temperature and adjust your baking time accordingly.

## 2. Baking Guidelines for Popular Polymer Clay Brands

Each polymer clay brand has its own specific recommendations for baking temperature and time. While these guidelines are usually similar, following the manufacturer's instructions is crucial for the best results.

**Fimo:**

- **Baking Temperature:** 265°F (130°C)
- **Baking Time:** 30 minutes per ¼ inch (6 mm) thickness Fimo is a popular brand of polymer clay that offers a wide range of colors and effects. It's important to bake Fimo clay at a lower temperature to avoid burning the colors. For thinner pieces, 15-20 minutes might be

sufficient, while thicker pieces may need the full 30 minutes.

**Sculpey:**

- **Baking Temperature:** 275°F (135°C)
- **Baking Time:** 15-30 minutes, depending on thickness Sculpey clay is known for its smooth texture and vibrant colors. It is one of the most commonly used polymer clay brands. Sculpey's recommended baking time varies depending on the thickness of your pieces. For thinner projects like earrings, 15 minutes may be enough, while larger pieces require up to 30 minutes.

**Premo! by Sculpey:**

- **Baking Temperature:** 275°F (135°C)
- **Baking Time:** 30 minutes per ¼ inch (6 mm) thickness Premo! is a professional-grade clay that is durable and flexible after baking. It requires a higher baking temperature than some other brands, making it ideal for creating

functional jewelry that needs to withstand wear and tear.

**Cernit:**

- **Baking Temperature:** 265°F (130°C)
- **Baking Time:** 30 minutes per ¼ inch (6 mm) thickness Cernit clay is a high-quality brand known for its porcelain-like finish. Cernit clay should be baked at a slightly lower temperature than some other brands, and longer baking times are necessary for larger pieces.

**Kato Polyclay:**

- **Baking Temperature:** 300°F (150°C)
- **Baking Time:** 30 minutes per ¼ inch (6 mm) thickness Kato Polyclay has a slightly higher baking temperature compared to other polymer clays. It is known for its strength and ability to hold intricate details, making it a popular choice for professional jewelry makers.

## 3. Adjusting Baking Times for Thickness and Layering

The thickness of your polymer clay pieces directly

affects how long they need to bake. Thicker pieces need more time in the oven to fully cure, while thinner pieces cure more quickly.

**Thinner Pieces:**

- For pieces that are less than ¼ inch (6 mm) thick, you can usually bake them for around 15-20 minutes, depending on the brand.
- If you're working with very thin sheets of clay or delicate details like thin charms or beads, check the piece around the 15-minute mark to avoid overbaking.

**Thicker Pieces:**

- For pieces thicker than ¼ inch (6 mm), it's important to bake them for at least 30 minutes, as thicker clay needs more time to cure properly.
- Be sure to follow the manufacturer's instructions for thicker pieces, as extended baking times are necessary to ensure the core of the clay is fully hardened.

**Layering Clay:**

- If you're stacking or layering clay pieces to create a thicker design, you'll need to increase the baking time to ensure the entire piece cures evenly. Check the manufacturer's instructions for any special guidelines when working with layered pieces.

## 4. Oven Calibration and Tips for Baking Success

Oven temperatures can fluctuate, and using an inaccurate oven can lead to uneven baking. To achieve the best results, it's important to ensure your oven is calibrated correctly.

**Use an Oven Thermometer:**

- An oven thermometer is essential for accurate temperature control. Even if your oven's built-in thermostat reads a certain temperature, it may not be accurate. Always use an oven thermometer to verify that the temperature is set correctly.

- Consider adjusting the oven temperature by 10-15°F if your oven runs hot or cold.

**Preheat Your Oven:**

- Preheating your oven ensures that the clay reaches the correct temperature right away. Place your polymer clay pieces in the oven after it has preheated and has stabilized at the correct temperature.

**Bake on a Clean, Flat Surface:**

- Bake polymer clay on a clean, heatproof surface such as an oven-safe ceramic tile or parchment paper. This will prevent any dirt or residue from affecting the appearance of your piece.
- A flat, smooth baking surface ensures even heat distribution, which can help avoid uneven curing.

**Avoid Overcrowding:**

- When baking multiple pieces, avoid overcrowding the baking sheet. Leave enough space between each piece for heat to circulate evenly.

**Cool Gradually:**

- After baking, allow your pieces to cool gradually. Sudden temperature changes can cause cracks, so let your clay cool in the oven with the door slightly ajar for about 10-15 minutes before removing it.

**5. Troubleshooting Common Baking Issues**

**Cracking or Breaking:** This can occur if the clay is baked at too high a temperature or too quickly. Always follow the recommended temperature and baking time for the specific brand of clay you're using. Avoid putting cold clay in a preheated oven.

**Burning or Discoloration:** If your clay turns brown or darkens during baking, it may be exposed to too much heat. Check the temperature with an oven thermometer to make sure it's correct, and reduce the baking time if necessary.

**Soft or Underbaked Pieces:** If your pieces feel soft or flexible after baking, they haven't fully cured. This usually happens if the baking temperature is too low or the baking time is insufficient. Increase the baking time or check that the oven temperature is accurate.

## COMMON BAKING MISTAKES AND HOW TO AVOID THEM

Baking is one of the most critical steps in creating polymer clay jewelry. Even with the best materials and intricate designs, improper baking can lead to undesirable results. Understanding the common mistakes made during the baking process and knowing how to avoid them will ensure that your pieces turn out perfect every time.

In this section, we will cover the most common baking mistakes in polymer clay jewelry making and provide practical tips for avoiding them.

**1. Baking at the Wrong Temperature**

One of the most frequent mistakes is baking polymer clay at the wrong temperature. Each brand of polymer clay has a specific temperature range for curing, and baking outside of this range can result in pieces that are too soft, brittle, or even burnt.

**How to Avoid This Mistake:**

- **Always use an oven thermometer:** Oven temperatures can be misleading, and the built-in thermostat in your oven may not be accurate. An oven thermometer will give you an exact reading of the temperature inside, ensuring that your clay is baked at the correct temperature.

- **Follow the manufacturer's instructions:** Every polymer clay brand has its own recommended baking temperature. Always check the instructions for the specific brand you are using and follow them carefully. If you are unsure, err on the side of a slightly lower temperature.

- **Preheat your oven:** Make sure to preheat your oven before placing your polymer clay pieces inside. This ensures that your pieces are exposed to the proper heat from the start of the baking process.

## 2. Not Baking Long Enough

Underbaking is another common mistake that can cause polymer clay to remain soft or flexible after baking. If your pieces are not baked long enough, they may feel firm to the touch but will be prone to breaking or bending under pressure.

**How to Avoid This Mistake:**

- **Bake according to thickness:** The baking time depends on the thickness of your clay pieces. For every ¼ inch (6 mm) of thickness, you should bake your piece for about 30 minutes. Thicker pieces will require additional time.

- **Use a timer:** Always set a timer when baking. It can be easy to forget about the clay, especially if you're working on other parts of your project. A timer helps prevent underbaking and ensures your clay cures properly.

- **Check for firmness:** After the recommended baking time, check your piece for firmness. Polymer clay should feel solid and slightly warm to the touch. If it still feels soft or flexible, bake it for an additional 10-15 minutes, checking regularly to avoid overbaking.

## 3. Overbaking and Burning

Overbaking polymer clay, especially at too high a temperature, can result in burnt or discolored pieces. This is particularly common with light-colored clays like white, cream, or pastel shades. Overbaking also causes the clay to lose its vibrant colors and may create an unpleasant odour.

**How to Avoid This Mistake:**

- **Lower the temperature for delicate colors:** If you're working with light-colored or translucent clay, try reducing the baking temperature by 10-15°F (5-8°C). These colors tend to burn more easily.

- **Monitor the baking process:** Check on your pieces periodically as they bake. While it's important to avoid opening the oven door too frequently (which can cause temperature fluctuations), it's okay to glance at your pieces through the oven window every 10 minutes to ensure they aren't burning.

- **Use an oven thermometer:** As mentioned earlier, using an oven thermometer is crucial for accuracy. If your oven runs hot, you may need to lower the temperature by a few degrees to prevent overbaking.

## 4. Inconsistent Baking Due to Uneven Heat Distribution

Many standard ovens have uneven heat distribution, meaning that some areas may be hotter than others. This can lead to uneven curing, where parts of your piece are perfectly baked, while others remain soft or undercooked.

**How to Avoid This Mistake:**

- **Rotate your pieces:** If you're baking multiple pieces on the same tray, rotate them halfway through the baking time. This helps ensure that all areas of each piece are exposed to the same temperature.

- **Use a baking tile or ceramic surface:** A flat, heat-resistant ceramic tile or baking sheet can help distribute heat evenly during baking. If you're baking larger pieces, this can help ensure the heat is absorbed uniformly across the surface.

- **Bake in small batches:** Instead of overcrowding the oven with too many pieces, try baking your jewelry in small batches. This allows for better airflow and more consistent heat distribution.

## 5. Placing Polymer Clay Directly on a Hot Surface

Placing raw polymer clay directly onto a hot baking sheet or a cold oven can result in cracking or deformation of your pieces. If the baking surface is too hot, it can shock the clay, causing it to warp or develop cracks. Likewise, starting with a cold oven can cause your pieces to bake unevenly.

**How to Avoid This Mistake:**

- **Preheat the oven:** Always preheat your oven to the recommended temperature before placing your clay inside. A sudden temperature change can cause the clay to crack or deform.

- **Use parchment paper or foil:** Always place your polymer clay pieces on a parchment-lined baking sheet or a clean piece of aluminum foil. This helps protect the clay from sudden temperature changes.

- **Avoid touching raw clay with your hands too much:** If you're handling the clay with your bare hands before baking, the oils and warmth from your hands can affect the consistency of the clay. Use clean, dry hands or wear gloves if you need to handle the pieces.

## 6. Not Allowing Polymer Clay to Cool Gradually

After baking, polymer clay needs to cool down slowly. If you cool it too quickly, the pieces may crack or warp due to thermal shock.

**How to Avoid This Mistake:**

- **Let it cool in the oven:** After the baking time is complete, turn off the oven but leave the door slightly ajar for 10-15 minutes. This allows the heat to dissipate gradually before removing the pieces.

- **Cool pieces on a flat surface:** After removing them from the oven, place your pieces on a flat, heat-resistant surface to cool completely. Avoid transferring them immediately to a cold surface, as the temperature change could cause cracking.

## 7. Using the Wrong Oven for Baking

Using a conventional kitchen oven can sometimes cause inconsistent results, especially if the oven has hot spots or inaccurate temperatures. Some makers prefer to use toaster ovens for polymer clay as they offer more precise temperature control.

**How to Avoid This Mistake:**

- **Consider a toaster oven:** Many jewelry makers prefer toaster ovens because they are compact and offer better temperature accuracy. If you're using a toaster oven, make sure to place your pieces in the center to avoid overheating.

- **Test your oven:** If you're using a regular oven, conduct a test bake on a small piece of scrap clay to check for even baking and accurate temperatures. This can help you assess your oven's performance before you bake your final pieces.

## SANDING, BUFFING, AND POLISHING FOR A PROFESSIONAL FINISH

Once your polymer clay jewelry pieces are baked and cooled, they are not yet ready for wear. To achieve a professional, smooth, and glossy finish, sanding, buffing, and polishing are crucial steps. These techniques enhance the appearance of your creations by removing imperfections, smoothing out rough edges, and adding shine. In this section, we will delve into the processes of sanding, buffing, and polishing, providing you with clear instructions to achieve a flawless finish every time.

## 1. Sanding: The Foundation for Smooth Surfaces

Sanding is an essential step in the finishing process. It removes the roughness caused by the baking process, smooths out fingerprints, and eliminates any small imperfections or uneven areas. The goal of sanding is to create a uniform, smooth surface that prepares your piece for the final buffing and polishing stages.

**How to Sand Polymer Clay:**

- **Start with Coarse Sandpaper:** Begin by using a coarse grit sandpaper (around 220-grit) to remove large imperfections and smooth out uneven surfaces. Use small, gentle motions, moving the sandpaper in a circular or back-and-forth direction. Avoid pressing too hard to prevent distorting the shape of your piece.

- **Progress to Finer Grits:** Once the larger imperfections have been smoothed out, move to progressively finer sandpapers (e.g., 400, 600, 800, and 1000 grit). Each finer grit will remove the scratches left by the previous one, resulting in a smoother surface. Work your way through the different grits, ensuring that you don't skip any steps, as this will leave noticeable lines or grooves.

- **Wet Sanding for a Smoother Finish:** For the smoothest finish, consider wet sanding. Wet sanding involves lightly wetting the sandpaper with water, which helps reduce friction, minimizes dust, and leaves behind a smoother surface. It also helps prevent the clay from overheating and cracking. Wet sand using grits as fine as 1200, 1500, or even 2000 for a glass-like surface.

**Tips for Sanding:**

- **Use a sanding block or sponge:** A sanding block or sponge can help keep the sandpaper even and provide more control, especially when sanding curved or detailed areas.

- **Sanding in Water:** If you opt for wet sanding, dip your piece into water frequently to keep it lubricated, preventing the sandpaper from clogging up with clay dust.
- **Be Patient:** Sanding takes time, especially for larger or more intricate pieces. Rushing through this step may result in an uneven surface that will be difficult to polish.

## 2. Buffing: Bringing Out the Shine

Buffing is the next step after sanding and serves to further smooth your piece, removing any remaining imperfections and enhancing its shine. Buffing is done with a rotary tool or by hand, depending on the effect you're aiming for. The buffing process removes the fine scratches left by sanding and gives your polymer clay jewelry that polished, shiny appearance.

**How to Buff Polymer Clay:**

- **Using a Rotary Tool:** A rotary tool, such as a Dremel, is the most efficient way to buff polymer clay. Attach a soft buffing wheel or a cotton wheel to the tool. Lightly apply pressure while moving the wheel across the surface of the clay. Use a medium speed and make sure the piece is always moving to avoid overheating any area.

- **Hand Buffing:** If you don't have a rotary tool, you can buff by hand using a soft cloth or a piece of felt. Apply gentle circular motions to the surface of your piece. This will still give your piece a nice sheen but may take more time to achieve the same level of gloss as machine buffing.

- **Buffing Compound (Optional):** For an extra high shine, you can use a buffing compound or wax. Apply a small amount of compound to the buffing wheel or cloth, then buff the surface of your piece. This will add a reflective layer and give your clay a glossy, professional finish.

**Tips for Buffing:**

- **Avoid overheating:** When using a rotary tool, ensure that you don't overheat the polymer clay during buffing. This can cause discoloration or deformation. Keep the tool moving and don't press too hard on the piece.

- **Test on scraps first:** Before buffing your main pieces, practice on a scrap piece of polymer clay to see how the tool works and get a feel for the correct pressure and speed.

## 3. Polishing: Achieving a Glass-like Shine

Polishing is the final step in the finishing process, and it's what gives your polymer clay jewelry that shiny, high-end, glass-like appearance. Polishing is a delicate process that enhances the appearance of your piece by giving it a smooth, lustrous finish that catches the light.

**How to Polish Polymer Clay:**

- **Polishing Compound:** Once your pieces have been buffed, you can further polish them with a polishing compound designed for polymer clay or a commercial product like Polycrylic or Future floor wax. Apply a small amount of the polish to a soft cloth, and use gentle circular motions to apply it evenly over the surface of your piece.

- **Buffing with a Soft Cloth:** After applying the polish, buff the piece gently with a clean, dry, soft cloth. This final step will bring out a deep, shiny luster.

- **Polishing by Hand:** If you prefer not to use a buffing wheel, you can still achieve a shiny finish by hand. Use a soft cotton cloth or microfibre cloth and apply a small amount of wax or polish to the cloth. Buff in small circles, working in sections to ensure even coverage.

**Tips for Polishing:**

- **Be Gentle:** Polishing requires a light touch. Rubbing too hard can cause the clay surface to become uneven or may even cause it to scratch.

- **Don't Overdo It:** It's important not to over-polish your pieces. A little polish goes a long way, and too much can leave a residue or cause a greasy look. Always use the smallest amount necessary for a beautiful shine.

- **Use a High-Quality Cloth:** A soft, lint-free cloth is essential for the polishing process. Microfiber cloths are ideal because they are gentle on the clay and help avoid leaving fibers behind.

**4. Adding Special Effects: Optional Finishings**

For an extra touch, you can add additional finishes to your polymer clay jewelry pieces after polishing to make them even more unique. These optional effects can enhance the overall look and feel of your designs.

- **Gloss Finish:** If you want an even shinier surface, apply a clear gloss finish over your piece after polishing. Some artists use a special polymer clay gloss or liquid clay. This will deepen the shine and protect the surface of your jewelry.

- **Matte Finish:** For a more subtle, elegant look, you can use a matte finish. This is particularly beautiful for earthy or rustic designs. You can use a matte varnish or polish to achieve this effect.

- **Antiquing:** For a vintage or aged look, apply an antiquing finish. This process adds depth to your design by highlighting texture and color variations, giving your pieces an antique, worn appearance.

**Conclusion**

Sanding, buffing, and polishing are the key steps in transforming your polymer clay creations from raw pieces to professional-looking jewelry. By carefully following the techniques outlined above, you can ensure that your polymer clay jewelry will not only look smooth and flawless but also have the depth and shine that makes it stand out. With practice, you'll develop your own methods and preferences for finishing your pieces, and soon you'll be creating jewelry that looks like it came from a high-end designer collection.

# CHAPTER 4. ADDING DETAILS: PAINTS, GLAZES, AND EMBELLISHMENTS

## USING ACRYLIC PAINTS, MICA POWDERS, AND METALLIC FOILS

Incorporating vibrant colors, shimmering effects, and unique textures is one of the most exciting aspects of working with polymer clay. Acrylic paints, mica powders, and metallic foils are three essential materials that can significantly elevate your polymer clay jewelry designs, adding depth, shine, and artistic flair. In this section, we will explore how to use these materials effectively to enhance your creations.

**1. Acrylic Paints: Adding Color and Detailing**

Acrylic paints are an incredibly versatile tool for polymer clay artists. They can be used to add intricate details, backgrounds, or even full-color designs to your clay pieces. Acrylic paint is known for its quick-drying properties, vibrant hues, and ease of use, making it perfect for enhancing polymer clay jewelry.

**How to Use Acrylic Paints:**

- **Base Coat or Background:** If you want to create a solid color or background for your piece, apply acrylic paint as a base coat. Use a flat brush to apply a smooth layer of paint directly onto the surface of your baked clay. Allow the paint to dry completely before proceeding with any further steps.

- **Detailing and Stenciling:** Acrylic paints are great for adding fine details such as designs, patterns, or texturing. You can use a fine-tipped brush to add tiny lines, dots, or shapes. For more intricate designs, use stencils to create clean and uniform patterns.

- **Blending Colors:** Acrylics are also excellent for blending colors on the surface of your clay. To create gradient effects or ombre designs, start with one color and gently blend it into another while the paint is still wet. Use a blending brush or sponge to smooth the transition between colors.

- **Layering:** To create depth in your designs, layer different colors of acrylic paint. After one layer dries, apply another layer of paint over the top, allowing the previous color to show through for a more dynamic effect.

**Tips for Using Acrylic Paints:**

- **Thin Layers:** Acrylic paints can be thick, so it's best to apply thin layers. Thick layers may take longer to dry and may crack over time.

- **Use Matte or Gloss Finish:** Depending on the look you're going for; you can finish your painted designs with either a matte or gloss varnish. A matte finish gives a more subtle, rustic appearance, while a gloss finish will make the colors appear more vibrant and shinier.

- **Test First:** Always test the paint on a scrap piece of polymer clay to ensure it adheres well and dries properly.

## 2. Mica Powders: Adding Sparkle and Depth

Mica powders are fine, shimmering powders that come in various colors, from metallics to vibrant pigments. When used on polymer clay, mica powders can add a sparkling, pearlescent effect that is perfect for jewelry designs. Mica powders can be applied both before and after baking the clay, allowing for flexibility in your artistic process.

**How to Use Mica Powders:**

- **Dusting Before Baking:** One of the simplest ways to use mica powders is by dusting them over your polymer clay before baking. Using a soft brush, lightly apply the mica powder over the surface of your clay. This will create a soft shimmer and enhance the colors of your piece. You can blend different shades of mica powder to create a more customized look.

- **Mica Powder as a Topcoat:** After baking your polymer clay, you can apply mica powder directly to the surface for a more intense shine.

Use a clean, soft brush to dust the powder onto the surface, and then gently buff it into the clay to set the shimmer. For a more dramatic effect, apply a light coat of clear glaze or varnish to lock the mica powder in place.

- **Mixing with Liquid Polymer Clay:** Mica powders can be mixed with liquid polymer clay to create a custom paint. This mixture can be used to paint intricate designs on your pieces before baking. It will produce a more even coverage compared to dusting.

- **Layering with Other Materials:** Mica powders look beautiful when layered with other materials, such as acrylic paints or metallic foils. This layering effect can create intricate textures and color gradients that make your jewelry pieces stand out.

**Tips for Using Mica Powders:**

- **Use a Masking Tape:** To avoid getting mica powder on unwanted areas of your piece, use masking tape to cover areas you don't want to decorate.

- **Work in Small Sections:** Mica powder can be a bit tricky to apply evenly, so work in small sections to ensure that the powder adheres well.
- **Avoid Over-applying:** A little goes a long way with mica powders. Applying too much can overpower your design and make the colors too saturated.

**3. Metallic Foils: Creating Bold, Shiny Accents**

Metallic foils are thin sheets of metallic-colored material that can be applied to polymer clay for a truly striking, reflective finish. Foils can add a rich, eye-catching effect to your designs, especially when used to highlight specific areas or create intricate patterns.

**How to Use Metallic Foils:**

- **Applying Foils to Fresh Clay:** If you want to add metallic foil to the surface of your polymer clay before baking, simply apply the foil directly to the uncured clay. Tear the foil into small pieces, place it onto the clay, and gently press down. The foil will adhere to the surface as the clay bakes, leaving behind a thin metallic layer.

- **Using Foils After Baking:** You can also apply metallic foils to your pieces after baking for more controlled designs. To do this, brush a thin layer of liquid clay onto the surface of your baked piece, then gently press the foil onto the area you want to decorate. Once the foil is applied, you can cure the clay again to set the foil in place.

- **Foil Sheets and Transfer Sheets:** Metallic foil comes in two main forms: loose foil sheets and transfer foil sheets. Transfer foil is more suitable for creating clean, detailed designs because it is adhesive on one side and can be transferred onto the clay using pressure.

**Tips for Using Metallic Foils:**

- **Be Gentle:** Metallic foils are delicate, so handle them carefully to avoid tearing or wrinkling.

Use tweezers or scissors to cut the foil into small pieces before applying it to your clay.

- **Avoid Overlapping:** When applying foil, try to avoid overlapping pieces, as this may cause unwanted streaks or uneven coverage.
- **Seal the Foil:** To prevent the foil from tarnishing or rubbing off, seal it with a layer of clear varnish or glaze after baking.

**4. Combining Acrylic Paints, Mica Powders, and Metallic Foils: Creating Multidimensional Designs**

One of the most exciting aspects of working with polymer clay is the ability to combine different materials to create stunning, multidimensional designs. By combining acrylic paints, mica powders, and metallic foils, you can produce jewelry pieces that have depth, shine, and texture. Here's how to use these materials together for maximum effect:

- **Layering Effects:** Start by painting your piece with acrylic paints to establish a base color or background. Once the paint is dry, apply mica powders on top to add shimmer and dimension. Finally, use metallic foils to accent specific areas or create focal points on your design.

- **Creating Contrast:** Use mica powders to add a subtle sheen to one area of your piece, while using metallic foils for bold highlights. This contrast will make your jewelry stand out and add visual interest.

- **Mixing Mediums:** Consider mixing acrylic paints with mica powders to create unique custom colors. The mica will give the paint a reflective, pearlescent finish, adding a layer of shimmer to your artwork.

## ACHIEVING A GLOSSY OR MATTE FINISH WITH GLAZES AND VARNISHES

The final finish on your polymer clay jewelry can dramatically impact its appearance and overall aesthetic. Whether you're aiming for a glossy, shiny surface or a more subtle, matte effect, the right glazes and varnishes can help you achieve your desired look while protecting your creations. This section will explore the different types of glazes and varnishes available for polymer clay and how to apply them for a professional finish.

## 1. Understanding the Difference Between Glossy and Matte Finishes

Before selecting a glaze or varnish, it's essential to understand the difference between glossy and matte finishes:

- **Glossy Finish:** A glossy finish gives your piece a shiny, reflective surface. This finish enhances the vibrancy of colors and gives a polished, professional look to the jewelry. Glossy finishes are particularly suitable for pieces that you want to appear sleek and smooth, like pendants or earrings with intricate details.

- **Matte Finish:** A matte finish provides a more subtle, understated appearance. It reduces the shine and reflects less light, resulting in a softer, more natural look. Matte finishes are ideal for rustic, minimalist, or vintage-inspired designs where a more muted, tactile texture is desired.

Both finishes can be achieved using different types of glazes and varnishes, and your choice will depend on the overall style you want to achieve.

## 2. Types of Glazes and Varnishes for Polymer Clay

Several types of glazes and varnishes are suitable for polymer clay. Each has unique properties that affect the final look and feel of your jewelry pieces.

**Polymer Clay Glazes:** These are specifically formulated to work with polymer clay and are the most common choice for achieving a professional finish. They are available in both glossy and matte versions, and they offer excellent adhesion, flexibility, and protection for polymer clay.

- **Glossy Glaze:** This type of glaze provides a shiny, reflective finish. It enhances the depth of colors and can make mica powders or paints shine. It's typically used on designs where you want the colors and details to pop.

- **Matte Glaze:** A matte glaze is designed to provide a non-shiny, smooth finish. It can be used to soften the look of a piece and reduce the shine. Matte glazes are also great for pieces where you don't want too much light reflection, such as more vintage or boho designs.

**Polyurethane Varnishes:** These are versatile varnishes that can be used on polymer clay to create a durable, protective finish. Polyurethane varnishes are often available in both gloss and matte versions and provide excellent long-lasting protection for your jewelry.

- **Glossy Polyurethane Varnish:** This varnish type gives a smooth, shiny finish that enhances the color and design details of your clay piece.

- **Matte Polyurethane Varnish:** The matte version of polyurethane varnish provides a more subdued, soft finish without any shine. It is excellent for creating a natural, understated look.

**Clear Acrylic Sprays:** Acrylic spray varnishes are quick and easy to apply. They come in both matte and glossy finishes and are ideal for adding a layer of protection to your designs. These sprays can be used for covering multiple pieces at once or for adding a light protective coating over intricate details.

**Renaissance Wax:** This is a popular choice for polymer clay artists looking for a light sheen and protective coating. Renaissance wax is applied in small amounts and buffed to create a subtle glossy finish. It's ideal for achieving a satin or glossy finish on smaller jewelry pieces.

**3. How to Apply Glazes and Varnishes**

Proper application is essential to achieve a smooth, even finish. The following steps will guide you through the process of applying both glossy and matte finishes to your polymer clay jewelry:

**Preparing Your Pieces:**

1. **Ensure Your Clay Is Fully Cured:** Before applying any glaze or varnish, make sure your polymer clay pieces are fully baked and cooled. Uncured clay will not hold the glaze or varnish properly, and it may result in an uneven or smudged finish.

2. **Clean the Surface:** Gently wipe your cured piece with a soft cloth to remove any dust, fingerprints, or oils. This will ensure that the varnish adheres properly and that no debris gets trapped in the finish.

**Applying the Glaze or Varnish:**

1. **Brush-On Application:**

- Use a soft, clean paintbrush to apply the glaze or varnish. Dip the brush into the glaze and gently apply an even, thin layer to the surface of your piece.

- For a **glossy finish**, be sure to use smooth, even strokes to avoid brush marks. Work in light layers to prevent drips or streaks.

- For a **matte finish**, apply the varnish in the same way but ensure that the application is consistent to avoid any shiny spots.

2. **Spray-On Application:**

- If you're using a spray varnish, make sure to spray from a distance of about 6-8 inches to avoid pooling or dripping.

- Hold the can at a consistent angle and spray in short bursts to cover the surface evenly.

- After spraying, let the piece dry completely between coats.

3. **Drying and Curing:**

- Allow your piece to dry thoroughly after applying each layer of glaze or varnish. Depending on the material, the drying time can range from 30 minutes to a few hours.

- Some glazes, such as polyurethane varnish, may require an additional curing period, so check the manufacturer's instructions for optimal drying times.

**Tips for Achieving a Smooth Finish:**

- **Multiple Thin Layers:** It's always better to apply multiple thin layers of glaze or varnish than a single thick layer. Thick layers are more likely to run, create visible streaks, or not dry properly.

- **Buffing After Drying:** For a higher sheen, buff the surface gently with a soft cloth once the glaze has dried. This will enhance the gloss and smooth out any imperfections.

- **Avoid Dust and Debris:** If applying multiple layers, ensure your work area is free from dust and other particles that can stick to the surface as the varnish dries.

## 4. Troubleshooting Common Issues

While glazing and varnishing are simple processes, you may encounter a few common issues along the way. Here are some solutions to ensure your finishes turn out perfectly:

- **Brush Streaks:** If you notice visible brush strokes after applying the glaze, it may be due to the glaze being too thick or the brush not being soft enough. Try using a higher-quality, soft brush and apply thinner layers.

- **Cloudy or Uneven Finish:** Cloudiness can occur if the glaze or varnish isn't applied evenly. Ensure you're applying thin, consistent layers. If you notice uneven areas, you may need to lightly sand and reapply the finish.

- **Tacky or Soft Finish:** If the glaze remains tacky after drying, it could be due to insufficient curing time or too much glaze applied. Allow the piece to cure fully before handling it, and avoid applying too many coats.

## 5. Choosing the Right Finish for Your Jewelry Design

When deciding whether to use a glossy or matte finish for your polymer clay jewelry, consider the following factors:

- **Design Style:** Glossy finishes often work well for contemporary or elegant designs, while matte finishes are more suited for rustic, vintage, or bohemian styles.

- **Color Impact:** A glossy finish can make colors appear more vibrant and bolder, while a matte finish can soften the tones and create a more subdued look.

- **Texture:** If your piece has a textured surface, a matte finish may highlight the texture without overwhelming it. On the other hand, a glossy finish will emphasize any textures and give a more polished look.

## INCORPORATING DRIED FLOWERS, BEADS, AND RESIN ACCENTS

Polymer clay jewelry offers endless possibilities for creative expression, and one of the most exciting aspects of working with this versatile medium is the ability to combine it with other materials. Dried flowers, beads, and resin accents can add stunning textures, colors, and dimensions to your pieces, making them truly unique. This section will explore how to effectively incorporate these elements into your polymer clay jewelry designs, with tips and techniques for achieving a harmonious and professional finish.

## 1. Using Dried Flowers in Polymer Clay Jewelry

Dried flowers are a beautiful, natural addition to polymer clay jewelry. Their delicate appearance and organic textures can be paired with vibrant clay colors or neutral tones to create captivating pieces. Here's how to use dried flowers effectively:

**Choosing the Right Flowers:**

- **Flower Types:** Not all flowers are suitable for embedding in polymer clay. The best flowers are those that are small, lightweight, and have flat petals. Some popular choices include lavender, daisies, roses, and violets.

- **Preservation:** Ensure the flowers are completely dried before incorporating them into your jewelry. Fresh flowers can introduce moisture into the clay, which may interfere with the curing process. You can purchase pre-dried flowers or dry your own by pressing them between pages of a book or using a flower press.

- **Size and Shape:** Smaller flowers or individual petals work best for polymer clay designs, especially when embedded in pendants, earrings, or brooches. Larger flowers may be challenging to work with unless you're making larger statement pieces.

**Embedding Flowers into Clay:**

- **Creating the Base:** Start by rolling out a thin sheet of polymer clay for your jewelry base. You can use a rolling pin or a pasta machine to get an even thickness.

- **Placing the Flowers:** Position the dried flowers directly on the surface of the clay. You can arrange them in patterns or clusters, depending on your design. Gently press them into the clay to secure them.

- **Covering the Flowers:** Once the flowers are in place, cover them with a thin layer of polymer clay. Use a roller or a clay blade to smooth the edges and ensure the flowers are properly encased without damaging them.

- **Baking the Piece:** Once your design is complete, bake the piece according to the manufacturer's instructions for your specific brand of clay. Be mindful of the temperature, as high heat can cause dried flowers to darken or burn.

**Post-Baking Tips:** After baking and cooling, you can add additional embellishments to enhance the look of your floral jewelry. For example, you can glaze the piece to make the flowers appear even more vibrant or apply a matte finish for a rustic effect.

## 2. Adding Beads to Polymer Clay Jewelry

Beads are an excellent way to add dimension and detail to polymer clay jewelry. They can be incorporated in various ways, from simple bead accents to full bead-encrusted designs. Here's how to work with beads:

## Types of Beads:

- **Seed Beads:** Small, round beads often used to create intricate patterns or to accentuate certain areas of a design.
- **Glass Beads:** Available in many shapes and colors, these beads can be used to add weight and shine to your jewelry.
- **Wooden or Metal Beads:** These beads bring an earthy or industrial aesthetic and can provide contrast against the smooth texture of polymer clay.

## Integrating Beads into Your Designs:

- **Bead Embedding:** Similar to dried flowers, beads can be embedded into polymer clay before baking. Roll out your clay and arrange the beads as desired. Gently press each bead into the clay to secure it in place. Make sure there's enough space between the beads for even curing and to avoid overcrowding.

- **Bead Stringing:** You can also use polymer clay as a base for beaded necklaces, bracelets, or earrings. Use clay to create pendant bases, links, or connectors, and then string beads onto jewelry wire or cord for a layered effect.

- **Bead Molds:** For uniformity, you can create custom bead shapes by using polymer clay bead molds. This method ensures consistency in size and shape, especially when making larger batches of jewelry.

**Baking the Design:** Once beads are placed and secured, bake your piece as usual, following the instructions for your specific clay. Beads made from glass or metal will generally not be affected by the heat, but it's essential to ensure that any polymer clay portions are properly cured.

### 3. Using Resin Accents in Polymer Clay Jewelry

Resin is a fantastic material to complement polymer clay designs. It can be used to create clear, glossy surfaces, or add depth and encapsulation for decorative effects. Resin accents also allow for additional creativity, as you can use them to add inclusions like glitter, pigments, or other small objects.

**Types of Resin:**

- **Epoxy Resin:** Epoxy resin is commonly used for jewelry making because it provides a high-gloss finish and is durable. It cures clear, which makes it ideal for encapsulating dried flowers, beads, or other materials within your polymer clay pieces.

- **UV Resin:** UV resin is a fast-curing option that is set using UV light. It is ideal for creating smaller pieces and can be applied directly on top of cured polymer clay.

- **Casting Resin:** This type of resin is generally used for larger pieces. It can be mixed with pigment, glitter, or small objects to create customized resin-filled polymer clay jewelry.

**How to Use Resin with Polymer Clay:**

- **Incorporating Resin into the Design:** Resin can be poured into shallow cavities or molds created in polymer clay. To create a pendant, for example, you can form a bezel around the shape and then pour resin into the cavity. After curing, the resin adds depth, creating a glossy, smooth surface.

- **Encapsulating Objects:** You can encapsulate small objects within the resin, such as tiny beads, sequins, or additional dried flowers. Make sure to arrange these elements within the polymer clay base before applying the resin.

- **Applying Resin Over Clay:** After your polymer clay piece has been baked and cooled, you can coat the surface with a layer of resin. This will give the piece a smooth, glossy finish and can be used to highlight the colors and patterns of your design.

111

**Curing Resin:**

- **Epoxy Resin:** Mix the resin according to the manufacturer's instructions, then pour it over or into the polymer clay design. Allow it to cure for the time specified by the resin brand, usually 24-48 hours, to ensure a clear, hard finish.

- **UV Resin:** If using UV resin, simply apply the resin and cure it under a UV light for the recommended time (usually 2-5 minutes).

## 4. Tips for Working with Dried Flowers, Beads, and Resin

- **Test on Scraps:** Before incorporating dried flowers, beads, or resin into your main jewelry piece, practice on scrap pieces of clay to understand how these materials react with each other and the curing process.

- **Don't Overcrowd:** While it's tempting to add multiple elements to your designs, keep in mind that too many embellishments can overwhelm the piece and detract from the clay's texture.

Focus on balance and simplicity for the most elegant designs.

- **Use Fine Detailing Tools:** To ensure precise placement of dried flowers and beads, use fine tools like tweezers, dental picks, or craft knives. This will help you position delicate elements without damaging them.
- **Sealing Resin:** After curing, if necessary, seal resin with a layer of glaze or varnish to add further protection and shine.

# CHAPTER 5: JEWELRY FINDINGS AND ASSEMBLY

## ATTACHING JUMP RINGS, CLASPS, AND EARRING HOOKS SECURELY

Jump rings, clasps, and earring hooks are the key components used to connect different parts of your jewelry design. Securing these findings properly ensures that your jewelry functions as intended, whether it's a necklace, bracelet, or pair of earrings. The strength and stability of these attachments are critical for the longevity of your designs.

### 1. Jump Rings: Essential for Linking Pieces

Jump rings are small metal rings that are used to connect various elements in jewelry, such as beads, charms, pendants, and clasps. They come in various sizes, materials, and finishes, allowing you to choose the perfect match for your polymer clay designs. However, to ensure they are securely attached and will not come undone with use, it is essential to learn how to open, close, and attach jump rings properly.

**Choosing the Right Jump Ring:**

- **Size:** Select jump rings that are appropriately sized for your project. Smaller jump rings (3mm-5mm) are ideal for delicate designs, while larger jump rings (6mm-10mm) are better for statement pieces or heavy charms.
- **Material:** Jump rings are made from various metals such as sterling silver, gold-filled, aluminum, or copper. The material should complement the aesthetic of your clay design and provide the necessary strength for your piece.
- **Shape:** While most jump rings are round, there are also oval and twisted jump rings, which offer added texture and a unique appearance. Choose the shape that best suits the design of your jewelry.

**Attaching the Jump Ring:**

- **Opening the Jump Ring:** Use a pair of pliers (preferably chain-nose or flat-nose pliers) to grip each side of the jump ring. Gently twist the ends apart rather than pulling them apart, as this will prevent the ring from losing its round shape. Twisting should be done in opposite directions (away from each other) to create a small gap.

- **Inserting the Components:** Once the jump ring is open, slide the elements you wish to connect (e.g., a charm or pendant) onto the ring. Be sure to insert the items that need to be linked before closing the ring.

- **Closing the Jump Ring:** Using your pliers, gently twist the ends of the jump ring back together. Make sure the ends are flush and properly aligned. There should be no gap, as even a tiny opening can cause the ring to come undone. After closing, inspect the jump ring carefully to ensure it is securely fastened.

## 2. Clasps: Securing Necklaces and Bracelets

Clasps are used to fasten necklaces, bracelets, and other jewelry pieces securely around the wearer's body. They come in many different styles, such as lobster clasps, toggle clasps, and magnetic clasps. Choosing the right clasp will depend on your design, the weight of the piece, and personal preferences.

### Types of Clasps:

- **Lobster Clasp:** A small, spring-loaded clasp that is one of the most secure types for necklaces and bracelets. Its shape resembles a lobster's claw and works well for delicate to medium-weight pieces.

- **Toggle Clasp:** Consists of two parts: a bar and a ring. The bar slides through the ring to secure the piece. Toggle clasps provide a decorative, stylish look and work best for heavier jewelry.

- **Magnetic Clasp:** These clasps use magnets to connect the two ends of the necklace or bracelet. They are convenient and easy to use, but may not be as secure as traditional clasps. Magnetic clasps are best used for lightweight jewelry or for pieces worn occasionally.

**Attaching the Clasp:**

- **Positioning the Clasp:** The clasp should be attached to the ends of the jewelry piece using jump rings. Be sure to use jump rings of appropriate size for the clasp and check that the ends of the chain or stringing material are securely attached to the clasp.
- **Securing the Clasp:** Whether using a lobster clasp or toggle clasp, attach one side to one end of the necklace or bracelet and the other side to the opposite end. Use pliers to secure jump rings tightly, ensuring they are properly closed to avoid breakage.
- **Testing the Clasp:** After attaching the clasp, gently pull on the jewelry piece to make sure it

is securely fastened. It is essential that the clasp stays in place and can handle the stress of regular wear.

## 3. Earring Hooks: Attaching Polymer Clay Earrings

Earring hooks are used to hang polymer clay earring designs. They come in various styles, including fishhook, leverback, and stud, depending on the design and comfort preference of the wearer.

### Choosing the Right Earring Hook:

- **Fishhook:** These are the most common type of earring hooks and feature a simple, open hook design that slips through the ear and fastens with a small rubber stopper to keep the earring in place.

- **Leverback:** This type of hook has a secure clasp that locks the earring in place once inserted through the ear.

- **Stud:** Earring studs are small posts that are attached to the back of the earring and then fastened with a small backing, ideal for lightweight earrings.

**Attaching the Earring Hooks:**

- **Inserting the Jump Ring:** For fishhook earrings, you'll need to attach a small jump ring to the polymer clay earring before securing it to the hook. Use the same method as described above to open the jump ring, insert the earring, and close the ring.

- **Attaching the Hook:** Once the jump ring is attached to the earring, simply thread it through the earring hook's opening. If you're using a leverback hook, you'll attach the jump ring directly to the leverback's closed loop. Make sure the hook is positioned securely, and the earring won't slip off.

# CHOOSING THE RIGHT STRINGING MATERIALS FOR NECKLACES AND BRACELETS

Stringing materials are essential for creating necklaces and bracelets that are not only beautiful but also durable. Choosing the right material depends on the style of the jewelry, the weight of the polymer clay components, and how flexible or rigid you want the piece to be.

## 1. Beading Wire

Beading wire is a popular choice for stringing polymer clay beads, pendants, and charms. It's a flexible, durable wire made from strands of stainless steel or nylon-coated metal, which can handle the weight of heavier pieces without breaking.

## Choosing Beading Wire:

- **Gauge:** The gauge refers to the thickness of the wire. A lower number represents a thicker wire, which provides more strength. For polymer clay jewelry, a wire with a gauge between

0.015" and 0.019" is ideal, as it's strong enough to hold your pieces without being too thick to fit through small beads.

- **Nylon-Coated or Stainless Steel:** Nylon-coated wire is flexible and resistant to fraying, making it ideal for stringing beads and pendants. Stainless steel wire is highly durable and strong, perfect for heavier or larger pieces.

**Attaching Findings to Beading Wire:**

- **Crimp Beads:** To attach clasps and other findings to beading wire, use crimp beads. Thread the beading wire through the clasp and then through the crimp bead. Using crimping pliers, flatten the crimp bead to secure it in place.

- **Crimp Covers:** After crimping, use crimp covers to hide the crimp bead and give your piece a more polished, professional look.

## 2. Elastic Cord

Elastic cord is an excellent option for making stretch bracelets or necklaces. It allows the jewelry to fit over the wearer's head or wrist and can be pulled on and off without the need for clasps.

**Choosing Elastic Cord:**

- **Thickness:** Elastic cords come in different thicknesses, typically measured in millimetres (mm). For a bracelet, an elastic cord with a thickness of 0.8mm to 1mm is ideal, as it provides enough strength while still being easy to work with.

- **Elasticity:** Ensure that the elastic cord you choose has good stretchability and returns to its original shape after being stretched. High-quality elastic cord will hold up over time and resist breakage.

**Securing Elastic Cord:**

- **Knotting:** For a secure knot, use a surgeon's knot, which is a double knot that ensures the ends of the elastic cord won't come undone. You can also use a dab of jewelry glue on the knot to reinforce the hold.

- **Covering the Knot:** Once you've tied the knot, cover it with a decorative bead or charm to hide it from view.

## 3. Thread and Cord

For a more textured look, consider using thread or cord for stringing beads and charms. Beading thread, leather cord, or waxed cotton cord offers flexibility and a unique aesthetic, perfect for bohemian or earthy designs.

**Choosing Thread or Cord:**

- **Beading Thread:** Made from nylon, beading thread is a strong and thin material ideal for delicate designs.

- **Leather or Waxed Cotton Cord:** Leather or waxed cotton cord is perfect for more rustic, boho-inspired jewelry and can add texture and dimension to your pieces.

## REINFORCING STRUCTURAL STRENGTH FOR LONG-LASTING WEAR

While polymer clay jewelry is durable, the strength of your pieces can be compromised by improper assembly or weak connections. Reinforcing your designs during assembly ensures that your jewelry will stand the test of time.

**1. Use Strong Adhesive for Connections**

For pieces that need additional strength, use a strong, flexible adhesive like E6000 or super glue. Apply the adhesive to joints, clasps, or connectors where polymer clay parts meet to ensure a strong bond.

**2. Double Up on Stringing Material**

For necklaces and bracelets, doubling the stringing material (e.g., beading wire) can add extra strength, particularly for heavier pieces. This will help prevent the jewelry from snapping or breaking with wear.

**3. Test Your Jewelry**

Before wearing or selling your jewelry, test its durability by gently tugging on the components and ensuring that the clasp and jump rings are securely attached. Double-check all connections to make sure that the piece can withstand regular wear without breaking.

# CHAPTER 6. FIVE BEGINNER-FRIENDLY POLYMER CLAY JEWELRY PROJECTS

## SIMPLE STUD EARRINGS: BASIC SHAPING AND BAKING TECHNIQUES

Creating simple stud earrings with polymer clay is an excellent entry point for beginners and a great way to explore the versatility of the medium. Stud earrings are a timeless and popular accessory, and when crafted with care, they can be both elegant and stylish. This section will guide you through the basic shaping techniques for polymer clay stud earrings, along with essential baking instructions to ensure your pieces are durable and professionally finished.

## 1. Choosing the Right Polymer Clay for Stud Earrings

For stud earrings, you want to select a polymer clay that is both firms enough to hold its shape and flexible enough to avoid cracking after baking. Brands like Fimo, Sculpey, and Premo are all excellent choices, as they offer a range of colors and textures suitable for jewelry making.

**Choosing the Right Clay:**

- **Opaque vs. Translucent:** Opaque clays are ideal for bold, vibrant stud earrings, while translucent clays are perfect for delicate, soft finishes or for incorporating materials like dried flowers or glitter.

- **Softness:** For beginners, consider using a softer clay (like Sculpey III) for easier shaping. If you're creating more intricate or structured designs, a firmer clay like Premo or Fimo Professional is recommended, as it holds its shape better.

## 2. Preparing the Clay

Before shaping your stud earrings, it is essential to properly prepare the polymer clay. Conditioning the clay helps to soften it and make it more pliable, preventing cracks during the shaping and baking process.

## Conditioning the Clay:

- Break off a small amount of polymer clay (usually a small ball for each earring).
- Knead the clay in your hands until it is soft and pliable. If necessary, use a pasta machine or clay roller to further soften and flatten the clay.

If the clay is too hard, you can warm it slightly by rubbing it between your palms or using a heat gun.

- If you're mixing colors, make sure they are blended thoroughly to create a uniform color or pattern.

### 3. Shaping the Earrings

The basic shape of stud earrings can be as simple or as complex as you like. Here are a few basic shaping techniques to get you started:

**Basic Round Studs:**

- Roll a small ball of clay (about the size of a marble or slightly smaller) between your palms until smooth.
- Flatten the ball slightly to create a disc shape. The thickness should be around 1/8 inch (3 mm) for a nice, sturdy stud.
- Use a small round cutter or your fingers to shape the edges evenly.

**Geometric Shapes:**

- **Square or Rectangle:** Roll out a thin slab of clay, then use a small knife or clay cutter to trim it into a square or rectangular shape. Gently round the corners for a soft finish or leave them sharp for a modern look.
- **Heart or Triangle:** To create unique geometric shapes, roll out the clay and cut it into the desired shape using a sharp blade or cutter. You can even use a small heart or triangle-shaped cookie cutter for more precision.

**Textured Studs:**

- Once you have the basic shape, you can add texture to your studs by pressing a textured surface (such as a piece of lace, a rubber stamp, or a textured mat) gently into the clay. This will create an interesting design, perfect for adding a unique touch to your stud earrings.

**Adding Detail (Optional):**

- If you want to add extra detail to your stud earrings, consider embedding tiny pieces of metal, beads, or glitter into the surface of the clay before baking. These accents can add visual interest to the earrings, making them truly unique.

## 4. Inserting Earring Posts

To turn your polymer clay creation into a stud earring, you'll need to insert an earring post. This is done before baking, so it becomes securely attached to the clay.

### Steps for Inserting the Post:

- **Position the Post:** Before baking the earrings, press the flat side of a metal earring post gently into the back of each clay disc. Be sure to place the post in the center of the earring, where it will sit comfortably on the ear.

- **Embed the Post:** Press the post into the clay just enough to leave a slight indentation. The post should not go all the way through the clay; just enough to stay securely attached after baking.

- **Ensure Alignment:** Check that the post is straight and centered. If the post is at an angle or off-center, it may cause the earring to sit awkwardly when worn.

## 5. Baking the Earrings

Baking polymer clay properly is crucial to ensure that your earrings have the strength and durability they need for long-lasting wear. Improper baking can lead to cracks, bending, or discoloration.

**Steps for Baking:**

- **Preheat the Oven:** Set your oven to the recommended temperature on your clay package (typically 265°F to 275°F or 130°C). Make sure the oven is fully preheated before placing your earrings inside.

- **Baking Surface:** Line a baking sheet with parchment paper or a ceramic tile to prevent the earrings from sticking to the surface. Place the earrings on the baking sheet, ensuring that they do not touch each other.

- **Bake According to Instructions:** Bake the earrings for the recommended time (usually 15 to 30 minutes, depending on the thickness of the clay). Make sure to keep an eye on the earrings, as baking time can vary slightly depending on the brand of polymer clay.

- **Post-Baking Cooling:** After baking, allow the earrings to cool completely before handling. Do not attempt to remove them from the baking sheet until they are cool to the touch.

## 6. Finishing Touches

After baking, you'll want to add any finishing touches to your polymer clay stud earrings.

## Sanding and Polishing:

- Use fine-grit sandpaper (220 to 400 grit) to smooth out any rough edges or imperfections on the surface of the earrings. Sanding will help to create a professional, polished look.
- For a shiny finish, you can buff the earrings using a soft cloth or a polishing pad.
- If you prefer a matte finish, skip the buffing step, or use a fine grit sanding block to give the earrings a more subtle texture.

## Adding a Glossy Finish:

- If you want a glossy finish, you can apply a layer of polymer clay glaze or resin. Be sure to apply the glaze evenly and let it dry completely before wearing or assembling the earrings.

## 7. Attaching Earring Backs

Once the earrings have cooled and finished, it's time to add the earring backs. These can be added by gluing a small rubber or metal earring back onto the post. You can also purchase pre-made earring backs with adhesive pads for easy attachment.

# MARBLED PENDANT NECKLACE: CREATING SWIRLS AND UNIQUE COLOR BLENDS

Polymer clay marbling is a stunning technique that creates beautiful, one-of-a-kind designs. Marbled pendants are perfect for beginners as they require minimal tools but yield professional-looking results. This section will guide you through selecting colors, blending techniques, shaping, baking, and finishing your marbled pendant necklace.

**1. Choosing Colors for a Marbled Effect**

The success of a marbled design depends largely on color selection. You can opt for:

- **Contrasting Colors:** For bold, striking marbling, choose colors that stand out against each other (e.g., black and white, blue and gold, or red and silver).
- **Analogous Colors:** For a subtle, harmonious look, select colors that sit next to each other on the color wheel (e.g., shades of blue and green, or pink and purple).
- **Neutral and Metallics:** Adding metallic or pearlized clay to neutrals can enhance the depth and shimmer of your design.

Start with two to four colors to avoid muddying the pattern.

## 2. Preparing and Conditioning the Clay

Conditioning polymer clay is essential to ensure smooth blending and flexibility.

- Knead each color separately until soft and pliable.
- Roll each color into a small log or thin sheet.

## 3. Creating the Marble Effect

**Basic Swirl Technique:**

- Take two or more logs of different-colored clay and twist them together.
- Fold the twisted log in half and twist again to intensify the pattern.
- Flatten the twisted clay with a rolling pin or acrylic roller to reveal the marbled effect.

**Feathered Marble Technique:**

- Roll out thin sheets of different-colored clays.
- Stack them on top of each other and roll into a log.
- Cut the log in half lengthwise and press both halves together to create a feathered effect.

Experiment with twisting, folding, and rolling until you achieve a pattern you like.

**4. Shaping the Pendant**

Once your marbled clay is prepared, you can shape it into a pendant:

- **Circular Pendant:** Use a round cookie cutter or bottle cap to cut out a symmetrical shape.

- **Teardrop or Oval:** Hand-shape the clay into an organic teardrop or oval using your fingers.
- **Abstract Shapes:** Use a craft knife or stencil to create asymmetrical, freeform designs.

Use a smoothing tool or your fingertips to refine the edges.

## 5. Creating the Necklace Hole

Before baking, you need to make a hole for the necklace cord:

- Use a toothpick, skewer, or small straw to create a hole near the top of the pendant.
- If you're using a jump ring or wire bail, embed it into the clay before baking.

Make sure the hole is large enough for your chain or cord to fit through comfortably.

## 6. Baking the Pendant

- Preheat your oven to the temperature specified on the polymer clay package (typically 265°F to 275°F or 130°C).
- Place the pendant on a parchment-lined baking sheet or ceramic tile.

- Bake for 15 to 30 minutes, depending on thickness.
- Let the pendant cool completely before handling.

## 7. Finishing and Polishing

After baking, sanding and buffing enhance the smoothness and shine:

- **Sanding:** Use fine-grit sandpaper (400 to 800 grit) to remove rough edges.
- **Buffing:** Rub the pendant with a soft cloth or a polishing wheel for a natural shine.
- **Glazing (Optional):** Apply a thin layer of polymer clay glaze for a glossy finish.

## 8. Assembling the Necklace

Once the pendant is complete, attach it to a necklace cord or chain:

- **For a jump ring attachment:** Open a jump ring with pliers, slide it through the hole, and attach it to a chain.
- **For a leather or waxed cord:** Thread the cord through the hole and tie adjustable knots.

- **For wire-wrapping:** Wrap a thin wire around the pendant's top for a more decorative look.

## MINIMALIST STACKING RINGS: SCULPTING AND FORMING THIN BANDS

Stacking rings are a stylish and versatile addition to any jewelry collection. Their delicate and minimalist design makes them perfect for everyday wear, and they can be customized in various ways. This guide will take you through the process of crafting thin polymer clay rings, from conditioning the clay to shaping, baking, and finishing for a durable and professional look.

### 1. Choosing the Right Polymer Clay for Rings

Since rings experience frequent handling and bending, selecting a strong and flexible polymer clay is essential.

- **Recommended Clays:** Premo Sculpey, Kato Polyclay, or Fimo Professional offer durability and resistance to breakage.

- **Avoid Brittle Clays:** Some softer clays may not hold up well under stress and may crack or break over time.

A translucent or neutral-toned clay can create a classic minimalist look, while metallic, marble, or textured designs can add character to your rings.

## 2. Conditioning and Preparing the Clay

- Knead the polymer clay until soft and pliable. This prevents cracks and ensures even shaping.
- Roll the clay into a thin, even rope about 2mm to 3mm in diameter for a delicate yet sturdy band.
- Keep the thickness consistent to ensure an even bake and prevent weak spots.

## 3. Measuring and Sizing the Rings

To achieve a proper fit, use a ring mandrel or a cylindrical object (such as a pen, dowel, or makeup brush handle) that matches the desired ring size.

- Wrap a thin strip of paper around your finger and mark where the ends meet.

- Measure the paper strip against a ruler to determine the correct size.
- Alternatively, use an existing ring as a reference.

## 4. Forming the Ring Shape

- Take the clay rope and carefully wrap it around your sizing tool.
- Cut off the excess clay where the ends meet.
- Smooth the seam by gently blending the edges together using your fingertips or a sculpting tool.
- Ensure the ring remains circular and free from distortions.

For **textured rings**, use a fine-grit sandpaper, a fabric imprint, or a texture mat before forming the band.

For **decorative designs**, you can add:

- **Tiny clay embellishments** like dots or geometric shapes.
- **Metallic foils or mica powders** for a subtle shimmer.

- **Hand-carved details** with a needle tool for a handcrafted effect.

## 5. Baking the Rings

- Place the rings on a ceramic tile or a curved surface (such as a glass bottle or ring mandrel) to maintain their shape during baking.
- Bake according to the manufacturer's instructions (typically 265°F to 275°F or 130°C for 30 minutes per ¼ inch thickness).
- Avoid overbaking, as this can cause discoloration, and underbaking, which weakens the structure.
- Allow the rings to cool completely before handling.

## 6. Sanding, Buffing, and Finishing

- Use fine-grit sandpaper (400 to 800 grit) to smooth out imperfections and refine the shape.
- For a glossy finish, continue sanding with higher grits up to 1500 or 2000.
- Buff with a soft cloth or a Dremel tool for a natural sheen.

- Apply a thin layer of glaze for added shine, or leave unglazed for a modern matte look.

## 7. Strengthening and Sealing the Rings

Since polymer clay rings undergo regular wear, reinforcing them ensures durability:

- Apply a thin coat of UV resin or epoxy for extra strength and a glass-like finish.
- If using a matte or satin varnish, ensure it's compatible with polymer clay to prevent stickiness.
- Let any sealant fully cure before wearing the rings.

## 8. Stacking and Styling Ideas

Minimalist stacking rings can be worn alone for an elegant look or layered in different ways:

- **Single Band:** A simple, classic ring in a neutral or pastel color.
- **Metallic Edge:** Apply a thin coat of metallic paint to the edges for a luxe finish.
- **Marbled Set:** Create a set of rings in different marbled hues for a coordinated stack.

- **Mixed Textures:** Combine smooth and textured rings for contrast.

## BOHO-INSPIRED DANGLE EARRINGS: LAYERING SHAPES AND ADDING TEXTURES

Boho-style dangle earrings are a beautiful and creative way to express individuality through handmade jewelry. These earrings feature layered shapes, intricate textures, and organic designs that blend natural and artistic elements. This project will guide you through crafting your own polymer clay boho earrings, from shaping and texturing to assembling and finishing.

# 1. Choosing the Right Polymer Clay and Materials

Polymer clay offers a wide variety of color and texture possibilities. For durable and lightweight earrings, select a strong yet flexible clay such as:

- **Premo Sculpey** (great for strength and flexibility)
- **Fimo Professional** (ideal for precise detailing)
- **Kato Polyclay** (durable and holds shape well)

**Other materials you'll need:**

- Clay roller or acrylic rolling pin
- Shape cutters or a craft knife
- Texture sheets, lace, or stamps for imprinting
- Jump rings and earring hooks
- Needle tool or toothpick for piercing holes
- Baking surface (ceramic tile or parchment paper)
- Sandpaper (400 to 1000 grit)
- Glaze or matte varnish (optional)

# 2. Conditioning and Rolling Out the Clay

Before shaping the earrings, soften and condition the clay by kneading it with your hands until smooth. This prevents cracking and ensures even textures.

- Roll out the clay to an even thickness of about 2mm to 3mm.
- If layering multiple shapes, keep them uniform in thickness for a balanced design.

## 3. Cutting and Layering Shapes

Boho earrings often feature organic and geometric layers, such as circles, teardrops, half-moons, and arches.

- Use clay cutters or a craft knife to create two large base shapes (e.g., teardrops or half-moons).
- Cut two smaller shapes (e.g., circles or ovals) to layer on top.
- Arrange the pieces on a flat surface to visualize the final design before attaching.

For more dimension, gently bend or curve some of the shapes before baking.

## 4. Adding Textures and Patterns

Textures bring a bohemian aesthetic to life. You can achieve different effects using:

- **Lace or fabric imprints** – Press lightly onto the clay for a delicate pattern.
- **Wood grain tools or stamps** – Create rustic, nature-inspired textures.
- **Embossing with needle tools** – Hand-carve small dots, lines, or tribal patterns.
- **Metallic foils or mica powders** – Dust over the surface for a shimmering effect.

## 5. Making Holes for Assembly

Using a needle tool or toothpick, carefully pierce small holes where the pieces will be connected with jump rings.

- Place holes at the top of the larger base shape for attaching the earring hooks.
- Add holes at the bottom of the base to dangle additional shapes, beads, or charms.

Make sure the holes are clean and even to avoid breakage during assembly.

## 6. Baking the Earrings

- Place the pieces on a ceramic tile or parchment paper to prevent distortion.
- Bake according to the clay brand's instructions (typically 265°F to 275°F or 130°C for 30 minutes per ¼ inch thickness).
- Let the earrings cool completely before handling to avoid warping.

## 7. Sanding, Buffing, and Sealing

After baking, refine the pieces for a polished look:

- Sand the edges with 400 to 1000 grit sandpaper to remove roughness.
- Buff with a soft cloth or Dremel tool for a natural sheen.
- For added durability, apply a thin layer of glaze or matte varnish, depending on the desired finish.

## 8. Assembling the Earrings

- Use jump rings to connect the layered pieces together, ensuring smooth movement.
- Attach earring hooks using pliers, making sure they are secure.
- Optionally, add wooden beads, metal charms, or tassels for extra boho flair.

## 9. Styling and Customization Ideas

- **Neutral Tones:** Use earthy colors like beige, terracotta, or muted greens for a natural boho look.
- **Bold Statements:** Combine vibrant patterns, marbled effects, or gold leaf for a unique design.
- **Mixing Materials:** Pair clay with wooden or metal accents for added texture contrast.

# STATEMENT CUFF BRACELET: ROLLING, EMBOSSING, AND BAKING A BOLD DESIGN

A statement cuff bracelet is a bold, eye-catching piece of jewelry that allows you to experiment with textures, colors, and intricate patterns. This project will guide you through creating a durable and stylish polymer clay cuff bracelet, incorporating embossing techniques for added texture and visual appeal.

## 1. Choosing the Right Polymer Clay

For a cuff bracelet, the clay needs to be strong and flexible to withstand bending without breaking.

- **Best Options:** Premo Sculpey, Fimo Professional, or Kato Polyclay are ideal for their durability.
- **Avoid Soft Clays:** Softer clays like Sculpey III tend to be brittle after baking.
- **Color Selection:** Bold hues, metallic shades, or marbled blends work well for a striking statement piece.

## 2. Preparing and Conditioning the Clay

- Knead the clay thoroughly until it is soft and pliable to prevent cracking.
- Roll out the clay using a rolling pin or pasta machine to an even thickness of ⅛ inch (3mm).
- To ensure a uniform bracelet width, use guides (such as wooden dowels or playing cards) on either side while rolling.

## 3. Creating the Bracelet Shape

- Use a flexible bracelet template or a paper strip to measure your wrist size.
- Cut a long, even strip of clay using a craft knife or a metal ruler.
- If adding layers or textures, ensure the base remains strong and not too thin.

## 4. Embossing and Adding Texture

Embossing and surface techniques enhance the bracelet's visual appeal.

- **Texture Stamps:** Press lace fabric, textured stamps, or carved wooden blocks onto the clay.
- **Hand-Carving:** Use a needle tool or stylus to engrave geometric, floral, or tribal patterns.
- **Mica Powder & Metallic Foil:** Lightly dust gold or silver mica powder for a metallic sheen.
- **Marbling Effect:** Twist and roll multiple colors together for a swirling, organic look.

## 5. Forming the Cuff Shape

- Drape the clay strip over a cylinder or bracelet mandrel (such as a glass jar or metal cuff form).

- Gently mold the strip around the form, ensuring even pressure to avoid distortion.
- Smooth out edges using a damp sponge or soft clay tool for a polished look.

## 6. Baking for Strength and Durability

- Place the clay-wrapped cylinder inside the oven to retain its shape.
- Bake at 265°F to 275°F (130°C) for 30 minutes per ¼-inch thickness, following the clay manufacturer's instructions.
- Allow the bracelet to cool completely before removing it from the form to prevent warping.

## 7. Sanding, Buffing, and Finishing

- **Sanding:** Smooth rough edges using 400- to 1000-grit sandpaper in a circular motion.
- **Buffing:** Polish the surface with a soft microfiber cloth or dremel buffing tool.
- **Glazing:** Apply a thin coat of matte or glossy glaze for extra protection and shine.

### 8. Customization and Styling Ideas

- **Metallic Finish:** Add gold leaf or metallic paint for a high-end look.

- **Boho Vibes:** Incorporate earthy tones and tribal-inspired carvings.

- **Abstract Art:** Use alcohol inks or acrylic paint for a unique, colorful design.

- **Personalized Touch:** Press in initials, symbols, or inspirational words before baking.

# CHAPTER 7. ADVANCED POLYMER CLAY TECHNIQUES

## MILLEFIORI CANE DESIGNS: CREATING INTRICATE PATTERNS

Millefiori, meaning "a thousand flowers" in Italian, is a traditional glasswork technique adapted for polymer clay. This method involves crafting intricate, repeating patterns within a cane—a log of layered clay that maintains its design even when sliced. Millefiori canes can be used for jewelry, beads, pendants, or surface decoration on larger polymer clay projects.

### 1. Understanding Millefiori Canes

A millefiori cane is a three-dimensional log of polymer clay that, when sliced, reveals a complex, symmetrical design. The key to success lies in precise layering, shaping, and reducing without distorting the pattern.

- **Basic Canes:** Simple geometric shapes, bullseye (concentric circles), striped designs.

- **Complex Canes:** Flowers, spirals, checkerboards, kaleidoscopic patterns.
- **Multi-Layered Canes:** Combining different smaller canes into a single large design.

## 2. Essential Materials and Tools

- **Polymer Clay:** Choose contrasting colors for a striking effect.
- **Acrylic Roller or Pasta Machine:** For conditioning and creating thin, even sheets.
- **Blade or Tissue Blade:** For clean, sharp slices.
- **Needle Tool or Toothpick:** For adjusting fine details.
- **Work Surface:** A smooth, non-stick surface like a ceramic tile or glass.
- **Ruler:** For accurate cutting and sizing.

## 3. Basic Millefiori Cane Construction: A Simple Flower Design

### Step 1: Preparing the Base Colors

- Select three colors: one for the petal, one for the petal outline, and one for the center of the flower.

- Condition each color thoroughly until smooth and pliable.

## Step 2: Creating the Petals

- Roll the petal color into a thick log, about 1 inch (2.5 cm) in diameter.
- Wrap it with a thin sheet of petal outline color (use a pasta machine for consistency).
- Reduce the cane by gently rolling it from the center outward, maintaining even pressure to avoid distortion.
- Cut the log into six equal sections to form the petals.

## Step 3: Forming the Flower Center

- Roll a small log of the center color (e.g., yellow for a sunflower look).
- Arrange the petal canes evenly around the center log, ensuring a tight fit.
- Fill any gaps with thin strips of a background color to maintain symmetry.

**Step 4: Reducing the Cane**

- Start from the middle outward, rolling gently while stretching evenly.

- Reduce the cane to the desired thickness (about ½ inch or smaller for jewelry).

- Cut into thin slices to apply onto beads, pendants, or other clay surfaces.

## 4. Advanced Millefiori Cane Techniques

- **Kaleidoscope Canes:** Combine mirrored segments of a millefiori cane for a symmetrical, mesmerizing effect.

- **Leaf Canes:** Layer shades of green and add vein details before reducing.

- **Geometric Canes:** Use precise striping and stacking for modern, abstract designs.

- **Gradient Canes:** Blend colors gradually to create a fading or ombré effect.

## 5. Using Millefiori Canes in Jewelry Making

- **Beads:** Wrap millefiori slices around round or oval clay beads before baking.

- **Pendants:** Press cane slices onto a clay base, then smooth with a roller.
- **Earrings:** Cut thin millefiori slices and shape them into lightweight earrings.
- **Bracelets:** Apply cane slices onto a rolled clay cuff for a unique design.

## 6. Baking and Finishing

- Bake millefiori-adorned pieces at 265°F to 275°F (130°C) for 30 minutes per ¼-inch thickness.
- Sand with 400- to 1000-grit wet/dry sandpaper for a polished finish.
- Buff and apply a glaze or resin coating for enhanced shine and durability.

## FAUX GEMSTONES AND NATURAL STONE EFFECTS

Polymer clay is a versatile medium that allows for the creation of realistic faux gemstones and natural stone effects without the need for expensive or rare materials. By using a combination of color blending, texturing, and surface treatments, you can achieve stunning results that mimic real stones such as turquoise, jade, marble, and even opals.

## 1. Understanding Faux Stone Effects in Polymer Clay

Faux gemstones and natural stone effects rely on techniques that replicate the appearance, translucency, and texture of real stones. The key to success lies in color layering, inclusions, and surface finishing to give depth and a natural look. Some popular faux stone effects include:

- **Turquoise** – A bright blue-green stone with black or brown veining.
- **Jade** – A translucent green stone with a smooth, polished finish.
- **Marble** – A white or colored stone with delicate veining.
- **Lapis Lazuli** – A deep blue stone with specks of gold or white.
- **Opal** – A milky or transparent stone with shifting colors.

- **Agate or Geodes** – Layered, semi-translucent stones with a natural, organic look.

## 2. Essential Materials and Tools

- **Polymer Clay** – Choose colors that match the stone you want to replicate. Translucent clay is useful for achieving depth.

- **Alcohol Inks or Acrylic Paints** – Used for veining and subtle shading.

- **Mica Powders or Pearl Ex Pigments** – Adds a shimmery, natural sheen to stones like opals and jade.

- **Chalk Pastels** – Crushed pastels provide speckling or color variations.

- **Fine Sandpaper (400-1000 grit)** – Used for smoothing and refining the final stone effect.

- **Resin or Gloss Glaze** – Adds a glass-like shine for realistic depth and brilliance.

- **Toothbrush or Needle Tool** – For adding stone-like textures.

### 3. Faux Turquoise Effect

Turquoise is known for its vibrant blue-green color with black or brown veining.

Step 1: Conditioning and Mixing Colors

Blend a mixture of blue and green polymer clay to match the turquoise shade. Add a small amount of white to soften the color.

Step 2: Creating Veining

Sprinkle finely crushed black chalk pastel over the clay and fold it gently to create thin, random veins. Use a needle tool to exaggerate cracks for a natural look.

Step 3: Shaping and Baking

Roll the clay into a bead or slab and bake according to the manufacturer's instructions.

Step 4: Finishing

Sand the surface with fine sandpaper and buff to a slight sheen. Apply a thin layer of glaze or resin for a polished gemstone appearance.

### 4. Faux Marble Effect

Marble has delicate veins and variations in color.

Step 1: Rolling and Layering

Roll out white polymer clay and layer thin strands of black or gray clay over it.

Step 2: Twisting and Folding

Gently twist and fold the clay several times to create natural-looking veins. Be careful not to overmix, as the veins should remain distinct.

Step 3: Smoothing and Baking

Flatten the clay and cut into jewelry shapes before baking.

Step 4: Finishing

Sand to a smooth finish and buff lightly. A matte finish often looks more realistic for marble.

**5. Faux Opal Effect**

Opals have a milky or clear base with shifting, iridescent colors.

Step 1: Creating the Base

Use translucent white polymer clay mixed with a small amount of pearl or mica powder for shimmer.

Step 2: Adding Color Shifts

Tear tiny pieces of iridescent cellophane or glitter and mix them into the clay. Layer different translucent shades to mimic natural opal variations.

Step 3: Baking and Finishing

After baking, coat the piece with a thin layer of resin to enhance depth and create the opal's characteristic glow.

## 6. Finishing Techniques for Realistic Stone Effects

- **Sanding and Buffing** – Most stones look best with a smooth, polished surface. Use progressively finer grits of sandpaper, then buff with a soft cloth.

- **Glazing or Resining** – For high-shine stones like opal or jade, a glossy glaze or resin coating will enhance the depth and color.

- **Matte Finishes** – Stones like marble or turquoise often look more realistic with a soft, matte finish rather than a high-gloss shine.

## SCULPTING FLORALS, LEAVES, AND NATURE-INSPIRED ELEMENTS

Nature-inspired polymer clay jewelry is a beautiful and timeless craft that allows artisans to capture the delicate details of flowers, leaves, and botanical elements in wearable art. By mastering sculpting techniques, you can create lifelike floral pendants, earrings, and charms with intricate textures and realistic color blending.

### 1. Understanding Botanical Sculpting in Polymer Clay

Nature-inspired polymer clay pieces focus on organic shapes, soft curves, and natural imperfections that mimic real flowers and foliage. To achieve a realistic effect, careful attention is given to petal shaping, vein detailing, and color gradients. Some of the most popular nature-inspired jewelry designs include:

- **Roses and peonies** – Layered petals with soft curling edges.

- **Daisies and sunflowers** – Simple, cheerful floral patterns with distinct centers.

- **Cherry blossoms and orchids** – Elegant and delicate designs with soft color transitions.

- **Leaves and vines** – Natural, flowing shapes with vein imprints for texture.

- **Mushrooms, acorns, and berries** – Whimsical elements inspired by forest botanicals.

## 2. Essential Tools and Materials

- **Polymer clay** – Choose colors suited to flowers and leaves, along with translucent clay for realistic effects.

- **Needle tools or toothpicks** – Useful for shaping petals and adding fine details.

- **Ball stylus tools** – Helps create smooth petal curves and natural indentations.

- **Leaf and flower cutters** – Speed up the process of creating symmetrical floral designs.

- **Veining or texture sheets** – Adds realistic patterns to leaves and petals.

- **Chalk pastels or mica powders** – Enhances color depth and adds a natural gradient.
- **Silicone mold (optional)** – Provides consistent shapes for flowers and leaves.

### 3. Sculpting Realistic Flowers

### Step 1: Forming the Base Shape

Start with a small ball of clay in your chosen flower color. Flatten it slightly to form the center of the flower. For roses and peonies, roll a tiny log and spiral it into a tight bud.

### Step 2: Shaping the Petals

- Roll out thin sheets of clay and cut small petal shapes.
- Use a ball stylus to gently thin the edges for a delicate, natural appearance.
- Curl and shape the petals by hand to mimic real flower structures.

### Step 3: Assembling the Flower

- Attach the petals one at a time, overlapping slightly to create a natural layering effect.

- For larger flowers like peonies, build multiple layers for fullness.
- Press gently at the base to secure each petal in place.

## Step 4: Adding Texture and Details

- Use a needle tool to add fine vein lines to each petal.
- Lightly brush the petals with chalk pastels to create depth and color variations.

## Step 5: Baking and Finishing

- Bake according to the polymer clay brand's instructions.
- Once cooled, sand lightly if needed and apply a matte or glossy finish depending on the desired effect.

## 4. Crafting Lifelike Leaves and Foliage

## Step 1: Rolling and Cutting the Leaf Shape

Roll out green polymer clay to the desired thickness. Use a leaf cutter or freehand cut a leaf shape with a craft knife.

**Step 2: Adding Veins and Texture**

- Press the clay onto a leaf texture sheet or use a needle tool to carve vein details.
- Gently curl the edges to give the leaf a more organic, lifelike appearance.

**Step 3: Enhancing Realism with Color**

- Dust the leaf with various shades of green, yellow, or brown pastels for natural variation.
- Highlight the veins with a slightly darker shade to add depth.

**Step 4: Baking and Finishing**

- Bake as per manufacturer guidelines.
- After cooling, add a satin glaze for a subtle sheen or keep it matte for a more natural look.

**5. Incorporating Botanical Elements into Jewelry Designs**

Once you have sculpted flowers and leaves, you can incorporate them into stunning jewelry pieces. Here are some creative ideas:

- **Floral stud earrings** – Small roses or daisies attached to earring posts for an elegant touch.

- **Nature-inspired pendants** – A cluster of leaves and flowers combined with beads or resin for a statement necklace.
- **Botanical charm bracelets** – Miniature flowers and leaves attached to a charm bracelet for a delicate, whimsical effect.
- **Dangle earrings with vines and blossoms** – Long, flowing designs with intricate foliage details.

## 6. Finishing Touches for a Professional Look

- **Sanding and Buffing** – Smooth out any imperfections and refine edges for a polished look.
- **Color Enhancements** – Use pastels, acrylic paints, or mica powders for realistic shading.
- **Glazing or Matte Sealing** – Choose a finish that complements the natural element you are replicating.

# INCORPORATING POLYMER CLAY WITH WIRE WRAPPING

Combining polymer clay with wire wrapping is a unique way to create intricate, artistic jewelry pieces that blend the versatility of polymer clay with the structural elegance of wirework. This technique allows for more dynamic designs, adds durability to clay pieces, and opens up creative possibilities for pendants, earrings, bracelets, and rings.

## 1. Benefits of Combining Polymer Clay and Wire Wrapping

- **Enhanced Structural Support** – Wire wrapping reinforces polymer clay pieces, making them more durable and long-lasting.
- **Versatility in Design** – Wire can be sculpted into decorative swirls, loops, and cages that complement polymer clay designs.
- **Professional Aesthetic** – The combination of clay and wire adds sophistication, making handmade jewelry look high-end.

- **Functional Integration** – Wire wrapping can create built-in bails, hooks, and clasps, eliminating the need for additional hardware.

## 2. Essential Materials and Tools

- **Polymer clay** – Choose colors that complement your wirework, or create faux gemstone effects for added elegance.

- **Jewelry wire** – Use 20 to 26-gauge wire in copper, silver, gold, or aluminium for wrapping.

- **Wire cutters** – Necessary for trimming wire to the desired length.

- **Round-nose pliers** – Helps create smooth loops and swirls.

- **Flat-nose pliers** – Useful for gripping and flattening wire wraps.

- **Needle tool or awl** – Creates small holes in the clay before baking to secure wire later.

- **Jewelry glue (optional)** – Helps reinforce connections between clay and wire.

### 3. Preparing Polymer Clay for Wire Wrapping

### Step 1: Designing the Clay Base

Decide on the shape and size of your polymer clay piece before introducing wire. Popular designs include:

- Oval or teardrop pendants
- Round or irregular cabochons
- Floral and organic shapes
- Beads or charms

### Step 2: Creating Holes for Wire Placement

Before baking, use a needle tool or toothpick to create small holes where the wire will pass through. This prevents cracks and ensures a secure attachment. If wrapping a cabochon, ensure the edges are smooth so the wire lays evenly.

### Step 3: Texturing and Baking

Add texture to your clay surface if desired, then bake according to the manufacturer's instructions. Allow the piece to cool completely before wrapping.

## 4. Wire Wrapping Techniques for Polymer Clay Jewelry

### Wire Frame Wrapping for Pendants

- Cut a piece of wire about 6–8 inches long and shape it around the polymer clay pendant.
- Use round-nose pliers to create a small loop at the top, forming a bail for stringing the pendant onto a necklace.
- Secure the wire by wrapping it around itself at the base of the bail.
- Add decorative spirals or swirls along the edges to enhance the design.

### Wire Cage Wrapping for Beads

- Insert the bead onto a 20–24 gauge wire and create a small loop at the base using pliers.
- Wrap the wire around the bead in a cage-like fashion, ensuring an even and secure fit.
- Finish with another loop at the top for easy attachment to earrings or necklaces.

**Embedding Wire into Polymer Clay for Secure Attachment**

For a seamless blend of wire and clay, partially embed the wire into the clay before baking:

- Shape the wire into loops or swirls and gently press it into the unbaked clay.
- Smooth over the clay edges to hold the wire in place.
- Bake as directed, ensuring the wire is fully secured within the clay.

**Weaving and Coiling Around Clay Elements**

For a more intricate look, weave thinner gauge wire around the clay piece:

- Wrap small coils around the base wire using a thinner 26-gauge wire for added detail.
- Intertwine multiple wires to create an elegant, textured effect around polymer clay pendants or rings.

## 5. Creating Jewelry Pieces with Polymer Clay and Wire Wrapping

### Polymer Clay and Wire Wrapped Pendant

- Create a polymer clay cabochon in a gemstone-like finish.
- Use a 20-gauge wire to form a frame around the cabochon, securing it with decorative loops.
- Wrap additional thin wire for added design elements.
- Attach a jump ring or wire bail for stringing onto a necklace.

### Wire Wrapped Polymer Clay Earrings

- Make small polymer clay beads or flat clay discs with texture.
- Use wire to wrap around the edges, forming a secure cage-like structure.
- Attach earring hooks or posts for stylish, elegant earrings.

### Bracelet with Clay Beads and Wire Links

- Handcraft small polymer clay beads and bake them.

- Use wire to create small loops on either end of each bead.
- Connect the beads with wire links, adding decorative spirals between them for a stylish bracelet.

## 6. Finishing Touches and Maintenance

- **Sealing and Coating** – Apply a thin layer of varnish to protect the clay and prevent the wire from tarnishing.
- **Polishing the Wire** – Use a polishing cloth to keep the wire looking shiny and professional.
- **Checking for Sharp Edges** – File down any rough wire ends to ensure comfortable wear.

www.ingramcontent.com/pod-product-compliance
Lightning Source LLC
LaVergne TN
LVHW020216011225
826732LV00009B/711